THE LAND WITHOUT SHADOWS

CARAF Books

Caribbean and African Literature Translated from French

Carrol F. Coates, Editor

Clarisse Zimra, J. Michael Dash,
John Conteh-Morgan, and
Elisabeth Mudimbe-Boyi,
Advisory Editors

ABDOURAHMAN A. WABERI

THE LAND WITHOUT SHADOWS

Translated and with an Introduction
by Jeanne Garane

University of Virginia Press
Charlottesville and London

Originally published in French as *Le Pays sans ombre,*
© Le Serpent à Plumes Editions, 1994

Excerpt from "Harvest of Hate" from *Idanre and Other Poems* by
Wole Soyinka © 1967 by Wole Soyinka. Excerpt from "Bearings" from
A Shuttle in the Crypt by Wole Soyinka © 1972 by Wole Soyinka.
Reprinted by permission of Hill and Wang, a division of Farrar, Straus
and Giroux, LLC, and Methuen Publishing, Ltd.

University of Virginia Press
Translation, foreword, and introduction © 2005
by the Rector and Visitors of the University of Virginia

9 8 7 6 5 4 3 2 1

LIBRARY OF CONGRESS CATALOGING-IN-PUBLICATION DATA

Waberi, Abdourahman A., 1965–
    [Pays sans ombre. English]
    The land without shadows / Abdourahman A. Waberi ; translated and
with an introduction by Jeanne Garane.
        p.   cm. — (CARAF books)
    Includes bibliographical references and index.
    ISBN 0-8139-2507-X (cloth : alk. paper) — ISBN 0-8139-2508-8
(pbk. : alk. paper)
    I. Garane, Jeanne, 1960– II. Title. III. Series.
    PQ683.A23P3913 2005
    843'.914—dc22   2005007875

CONTENTS

FOREWORD

Nuruddin Farah

In the summer of 1990, I had the fortune of meeting the late Swiss novelist and dramatist Friedrich Dürrenmatt in the airport lounge in Budapest, where we had attended a literary conference earlier in the week. He asked if I was writing a novel. When I replied in the affirmative, Mr. Dürrenmatt—describing himself as a writer who hungers after stories in the way a child might hunger after sweets—requested that I tell him a summary of the story I meant to tell, which he hoped would help us pass the time profitably. I obliged, unexpectedly bettering my own expectations, for I jumped ahead of myself, plunging further into areas of the narrative that I had neither charted out until then nor fleshed out in writing. Ever so charming, Mr. Dürrenmatt was polite enough to hear me out without a single interruption. Moreover, he was very attentive to the detailed nuance of my telling—never once raising in me the suspicion of showing little or no interest. When I was done, his breathing quickened the way the breathing of the feeble-hearted do. Then he surprised me by sitting upright as he readied to speak. In fact, he said, "Why, Mr. Farah, should I expend the little time at my disposal and my precious energy in reading your novel? What is in it for me? What, in short, will I gain from it?"

I doubt that I gave a satisfactory answer to Mr. Dürrenmatt's provocative question, the question of an old writer cynically testing a younger writer's mettle. Given the chance to respond to it—not about my writing, but about someone else's output—I shall push the yardsticks aside for a start, because it is altogether a different matter when we are dealing with the writings of others, and shall act in an uninhibited way and express my strong feeling, convinced that I will reach up to the height of Mr. Dürrenmatt's question, which has towered over me since that day.

FOREWORD

To what purpose, indeed, does one read a book? What manner of benefits will accrue to one who expends time and energy in reading a text? What subliminal and emotional reasons commit me to the act of reading the texts of, say, the Djiboutian short story writer Abdourahman A. Waberi, poet, novelist, and essayist? The answer is simple: because I admire his texts greatly, because I receive immeasurable enjoyment from reading them, and because in the eyes of Djiboutian posterity, Waberi will be remembered for having brought the story of his nation to life. Moreover, the series of texts contained in this collection inspire me in ways that energize my memory, awakening it.

It is both a pleasure and an immense honor to present this collection of stories, written in exquisite French by Abdourahman A. Waberi, ably translated into English by Jeanne Garane, which have made their way into the larger and more competitive world and cultivated a special kind of intimacy with their readers.

Djibouti—with its coveted position at the entrance to the Red Sea which offers it a strategic significance disproportionate to its smallness—is siesta country, in the sense that it is tropically hot all year round, and humid, thanks to the pervasiveness of the sea and the salt in the air. The people of this tiny Horn of Africa country are an outdoors people, fun loving, generous, and with the outlook of a polyglot nation, whose cultures and traditions are anchored in cosmopolitanism.

There is something apocalyptic about the landscape, which also boasts an outcrop of geological richness seldom seen anywhere else in the world.

Abdourahman A. Waberi's writing is a perfect match for the country it portrays: brief, wealthy in its cosmopolitan idiom, and concise in its deployment of words, metaphors, parables, folktales, and images. In addition to the deliberateness, there is a kind of daring: this advances the telling of his tales. Of the stand-alone tales, imbued with the flavors of fables, my favorite, which I read and reread, is "The Seascape Painter and the Wind Drinker." I find it bold in its abundant strokes of genius. It would be worth quoting at length from this story about three men, if only we had sufficient space. This is how it begins: "One paints the sea as a vocation; the other drinks the wind out of dereliction; both are unemployed. Badar and Dabar have as their friend a sculptor of dreams who is just as ragged as they are." I delight in its twists and turns and in the delicate handling of the material, at once playful and serious.

Waberi cultivates to perfection the idea of describing his country accurately and countering the exotic images of Djibouti in literature written by French writers. Another favorite vignette of mine is about the railroad, which links Djibouti to Addis Ababa, crossing "the land of reality and of dreams." His poetic prose in French is clear, concise, and not at all encumbered with the rhetorical devices of his mother tongue, Somali. Yet, there is evidence of his Somaliness everywhere in the text—now alluded to in the parables that he rewrites, making them his own, now hidden as hunches or secret messages in the form of symbols that his conationals can appreciate, and now acknowledged with a nod of his head as a tribute to his provenance. In fact, every now and then Waberi surrenders his creative energy wholly to the Somali side of him: rhetorical, lyrical, metaphor based, and fond of deploying parables as a mode of literary composition.

A modest man, Abdourahman A. Waberi says, "I am a short story writer and a poet. I believe in more rapid strokes and in concision, not seven-hundred-page novels with well-depicted characters." He is much more than that. To my mind, he is one of the most accomplished writers of his generation, and one of its most urbane artisans, highly original in his approach, humorous, generous, and very entertaining.

TRANSLATOR'S ACKNOWLEDGMENTS

I would like to thank Abdourahman A. Waberi for his close collaboration on this translation. (He provided the text for all of the footnotes, in addition.) I am also grateful to Nuruddin Farah for his participation in this project, to Carrol Coates for his excellent editorial eye and his uncanny ability to choose *le mot juste*, and to Anny Dominique Curtius of the University of Iowa for her help with the Creole sections of "The Dasbiou Mystery." Thanks also go to the College of Liberal Arts at the University of South Carolina for a grant that funded a trip to meet with and interview Mr. Waberi; to William Edmiston, Chair of the Department of Languages, Literatures, and Cultures at the University of South Carolina, for supporting this endeavor; and to my colleague Freeman Henry for his valuable advice. I am most indebted to my dear friend and colleague Dianne Johnson for her photograph of Mr. Waberi and to Mr. Thomas Goisque for the cover photograph. Last, but not least, loving thanks to my family for their constant patience and support.

INTRODUCTION

I still traffic in poetic material.

—Abdourahman A. Waberi

Djibouti: The Land without Shadows

First published in 1994, *Le Pays sans ombre* is the original French title of the present collection of seventeen short stories by Abdourahman A. Waberi. It could be said that these short stories are like so many sparkling gems, but it would be more fitting to compare them to the sharp fragments of volcanic rock that form the bedrock of Djiboutian territory: compact and incisive, they radiate with the intensity of a scorching sun.

"Le pays" or "land" in question is indeed the "miniature republic" of Djibouti, as Waberi calls it in one of his poems,[1] a country ranging 8,450 square miles, an area about the size of the state of Massachusetts. Near the Suez Canal and across the Red Sea from Yemen, strategically located on the shipping routes between the Mediterranean Sea and the Indian Ocean, Djibouti lies on the west side of Bab-el-Mandeb (The Gate of Tears), a strait that connects the Red Sea and the Gulf of Aden. Often described as a "land of encounters" at the crossroads of Africa, the Middle East, and Asia, this "pocket-sized country," to use another of Waberi's expressions, is bordered by Eritrea to the north, Ethiopia to the west and south, and Somalia to the southeast.

The French presence in Djibouti dates from its purchase of the port of Obock in 1862, followed by its definitive acquisition of the territory in 1896. Called "la Côte française des Somalis," then "le Territoire français des Afars et Issas" while it was a French colony, and finally "Djibouti" after obtaining its independence from France in 1977, the country is inhabited by the nomadic Afar people,[2] the Issa (one of several nomadic ethnic Somali clans living in the region), Arabs, Europeans, French military personnel stationed at their base there, and American soldiers sent for antiterrorist training in the torrid Djiboutian desert and to patrol the waters of the Gulf of Aden.

Although the territory has been coveted by the Ottoman Turks, Ethiopia, France, and Somalia under the late dictator Siad Barre, until recently the importance of the country has been ignored. With characteristic irony, Abdourahman A. Waberi traces the roots of what he calls this "maddening" tendency in *Rift, routes, rails,* his third collection of short stories:

> 1882. A French navigator, Denis de Rivoyre, reaches Obock aboard the Séverin, a seven-ton steamship. This little fishing port on the Red Sea was nothing but a brief port of call . . . Obock, just time enough for a quick stop to refuel coal and water. From this time on, long-distance travelers had gotten into the maddening habit of just passing through this bit of undesirable land. So people only stop by. Stay for a longer length of time? Never. And yet, we are at a crossroads, and not at the ends of the earth, if such a place exists. . . . (13–14)

While Djibouti has indeed been called a "crossroads," it has just as frequently been compared to an inferno because of its inhospitable environment.[3] Indeed, its nomads struggle against the harsh natural environment for survival, while many of the urban inhabitants, often former nomads, live in poverty. The second part of the original French title of the present collection, "sans ombre," presumably refers to the sweltering climate. Upon visiting Djibouti in 1971, just six years before it acquired its independence, the French novelist Romain Gary suggested stopping at the place "if hell tempts you," for "the one hundred thousand extinct volcanoes here make this region of Africa a black chaos of charred rock" (14). To him the inhabitants appeared "to be made of shadows" (15), and their choice to inhabit this geographically hostile (44) land unfathomable.

Still, the translator ponders the ambiguity of the French title: does "sans ombre" refer to the fact that in Djibouti there is scarcely any shade, given the sparseness of any vegetation that could shelter the tough but embattled inhabitants of this unforgiving land? One has only to recall the implausible postcard images of goats grazing on—not under—the rare acacia trees, since the rocky earth offers little forage. In his poem "Acacia," Abdourahman A. Waberi translates this image into words:

> prince of the countryside
> on your roof a goat moves
> slender
>
> a horde of ants caresses your roots
> while the goat grazes on your finest
> leaves
> the ants take shelter from the sun[4]

In 1884 Pierre Loti, the French novelist and travel writer, who had arrived in the port of Obock from Aden, was less kind when he described the acacias or mimosas in "Obock, for a Day," as "sickly-looking umbrella-shaped shrubs with scanty, meager foliage . . . a sort of thorny parasol, leaning to the right or left on their slender trunks . . . a mimosa which yields nothing, is of no use, does not even cast a shade" (180). And Loti was seeking shade, for he had landed in "one of the hottest spots on earth. It was as yet hardly eight in the morning and our cheeks and temples already smarted with a scorching sensation as though we were too close to a fierce fire" (171).

Or perhaps "sans ombre" refers to a land "without shadows," as Loti further observed when the murderous rays of the sun drilled into him at high noon like so many shards of splintered glass (to borrow an image from Waberi himself) and his body cast no shadow as though it had ceased to exist:

> Soon it is noon. At this hour, white men never stir out of doors. . . . Our shoulders under our white linen clothing

sting with the feeling of being actually burnt. As we go, we cast no shadow, no more than a circular spot under our feet: the sun is exactly overhead, and its fierce rays fall vertically to the ground. Not a sign of life; everything is stricken by the heat. (182–83)

To imagine this infernal heat, one need merely evoke the simplest but most improbable of tourist souvenirs: a green glass bottle stretched and twisted after having been left out in the Djiboutian sun.

The French word "ombre" evokes both "shade" and "shadow." But since a translator must choose, I have chosen the phrase "without shadow" to translate "sans ombre," since it renders better both the absence of shelter from the sun and the struggle to exist. The absence-presence of Waberi's Djiboutians that lies at the heart of each of the author's short stories about his homeland and the people who live there, be they madmen, poets, artists, French colonists, pseudointellectuals, young women, aspiring politicians, famished refugees from the Somali civil war, khat chewers, nomads struggling to survive in Djibouti's ruthless natural environment, or tramps living (and dying) in Balbala, the "great shantytown of rock and corrugated metal that stretches to the south of the capital," as Waberi describes it in his novel of the same name (*Balbala* 14).

Abdourahman A. Waberi and the "New Generation" of Francophone African Writers

Born in 1965 in a shantytown, the "lower city" of Djibouti's Quartier 6, Abdourahman A. Waberi was nevertheless able to attend primary and secondary school, where instruction was, and still is, carried out in French. After graduating from high school in 1985, Waberi left Djibouti for France. He studied English at the University of Caen, and completed a degree in English at the University of Dijon, where he wrote a thesis on the work of Somali novelist Nuruddin Farah. He now resides in Caen, where he teaches English and writes. In addition to his activities as a fiction writer and poet, Mr. Waberi is a regular contributor to *Le Monde Diplomatique,* is a member of the international jury for the Ulysses Award for Excellence in the Art of Reportage, and has served as a literary adviser to Le Serpent à Plumes publishing house. He regularly contributes articles to a number of other literary journals, including *Lettre Internationale* and *Notre Librairie.*

Mr. Waberi is one of a handful of francophone writers of fiction to have emerged from the small former French colony of Djibouti.[5] His work has already earned international recognition, as shown by the number of awards he has received. In 1994 the Belgian Royal Academy of French Language and Literature and the Henri Cornélus Foundation awarded the Grand Prize for the Francophone Short Story to *Le Pays sans ombre.* The Paris Académie des Sciences d'Outre-Mer awarded the volume the Prix Albert Bernard in the same year. In 2000 J. Michael Dash's translation of "The Gallery of the Insane" from the collection was short-listed for the Caine Prize in African Fiction. In addition to the prizes awarded to *Le Pays sans ombre,* his second collection of short stories, *Cahier nomade* (Nomadic Notebook), won the Grand Prix Littéraire d'Afrique Noire in 1996. Mr. Waberi's novel *Balbala* has also won a number of literary prizes.

In 1999 Mr. Waberi was one of ten African writers invited to participate in the project entitled "Rwanda: Ecrire par devoir de mémoire" (Rwanda: writers and the duty to remember). This group spent two months in that country and wrote about the aftermath of the 1994 genocide there. The result was *Moisson de crânes: Textes pour le Rwanda* (Harvest of Skulls: Stories and Essays for Rwanda). Both Mr. Waberi's third collection of short stories, *Rift, routes, rails,* and his second novel, *Transit,* about civil war in Djibouti and forced migration to France, appear in Gallimard's series "Continents Noirs."

Abdourahman A. Waberi is often placed among the so-called New Generation of francophone African writers who emerged in the 1990s. In an essay entitled "Les Enfants de la Postcolonie" ("Children of the Postcolony"), Mr. Waberi calls his generation "transcontinental," noting that all twenty writers included in this group were born after 1960 (the year so many francophone African countries obtained their independence from France). They live in France and hold university diplomas.[6] Citing the example of Calixthe Beyala, who has called herself a "Franco-Cameroonian," Waberi asserts that these writers have no qualms about calling themselves "Franco-somethings" (12). Moreover, Waberi remarks on the extent to which the "theme of the return to the native land has practically disappeared from the landscape of the African novel," noting that "it is the opposite theme, the arrival of the African in France that is popular in the work of the young writers" (13). Such is the case at the beginning of the novel *Transit,* where the main characters have landed at Roissy–Charles de Gaulle airport in Paris as refugees from the 1991–94 civil war that erupted in Djibouti between members of the Front for the Restoration of Unity and Democracy (FRUD) and the Djiboutian government. Nevertheless, with the exception of some stories in *Rift, routes, rails,* the author's native land continues to occupy center stage even in *Transit,* where flashbacks to Djibouti constitute much of the novel's content.

When I asked him in an interview whether he considers himself a "francophone" writer, Mr. Waberi responded,

> . . . if I'm "francophone" when I write in French, then I am one. I would say that I am a French-language writer. Now, if "francophonie" is the space of the imaginary, of words, of culture open to whoever can align two or three words in French on a page, yes, in that case I would be a francophone, but also someone from a certain new France. Sometimes I define myself as a neo-Frenchman, although in general I haven't written a single line about France, but I live there. To be honest, I am a French citizen, I pay taxes there, my children were born there, and their mother is French. This new France interests me potentially. So, yes and no. (139)[7]

"Yes and no." The ambivalence of this phrase captures the unresolved and unsolvable issue of the so-called language question, debated, as Waberi puts it in an essay entitled "Comment j'ai écrit mes livres et autres considérations sommaires" ("How I Wrote My Books and Other Summary Considerations"), "*ad nauseam* by our elders (and by us today), although it has never been settled. And it cannot be." Should one write in one's first tongue, Somali in this case, or in the language of the occupier? While novelists and poets of preceding generations may have felt guilty about writing in French, Waberi asserts that this "feeling of guilt seems to have disappeared, in particular with the young writers of my generation." In fact, he writes, while "the father's language is not always equipped to express his son's world," the language of the occupier "harbors unsuspected privileges" (937).

The Art of the Fragment

Just what are the "unsuspected privileges" concealed in the language of the occupier? Waberi is not explicit. But by choosing to write in French, he inserts a Djiboutian point of view into an international discussion that was begun in antiquity by travelers from places like ancient Egypt, Greece, Rome, and China who knew the Horn of Africa as the land of frankincense and myrrh. For different reasons, that discussion continues to this day, as military planners consider Djibouti's strategic proximity to the Persian Gulf. But because *The Land without Shadows* is one of the first literary works to portray Djibouti from a Djiboutian point of view, this discussion has now become a conversation between Djiboutians, who have had no say, and those who have said so much about the place. As Waberi himself puts it,

> Djibouti has often been the subject, or worse, the object, even the pretext for an entire area of French literature. . . . Nevertheless that gaze and what it produced is now finished. There are no Djiboutians [in that gaze]. . . . To live, a Djiboutian does not need to read Loti, Rimbaud or [Albert] Londres. . . . As for myself, as a writer, I work on

that particular memory, and at times I try to provide what has been called a "native gaze." But that only interests people who are familiar with literary history. ("Comment faire exister" 145–46)

Indeed, Djibouti and its environs have long been a venue for travelers who wrote of their adventures there, and not always in a positive light. Today, the history and people of the Horn of Africa are often reduced to a single reference: "Somalia." The name has become synonymous with the disastrous outcome of the 1992–93 American military mission known as "Operation Restore Hope," when two American Black Hawk helicopters were shot down over Mogadishu by gunmen loyal to Mohammed Farah Aideed, and the body of an army ranger was dragged through the streets of Mogadishu. Eighteen American soldiers and hundreds of Somali fighters and civilians alike were killed.[8]

Now, *The Land without Shadows* adds a Djiboutian voice to discourses on the Horn of Africa. Indeed, writes Jean-Claude Guillebaud, "it has now become impossible to write about Djibouti as we did in the not-so-distant past when its real inhabitants were mute" (31). Comparing his situation to that of Nuruddin Farah, who writes about Somalia in English, Mr. Waberi explains,

> I who am in exile, I have become, without any pretensions I believe, a bit of a spokesman for Djibouti. It wasn't planned that way. One becomes the bearer of a nation, of a culture that one must make exist on "planet literature," but one must oneself go off and be a nomad elsewhere. That's the paradox. ("Comment faire exister" 140)

Drawing on the Somali/Djiboutian oral tradition for bits of legend, proverbs, music, poetry, and history, and weaving them together with references to world writers like Chinua Achebe, Charles Baudelaire, Samuel Beckett, Rabah Belamri, Aimé Césaire, Louis Calaferte, Dante Alighieri, Assia Djebar,

Cyprian Ekwensi, Nuruddin Farah, Rachid Mimouni, Tierno Monénembo, Emile Ollivier, Arthur Rimbaud, L. S. Senghor, William Shakespeare, Wole Soyinka, Tchicaya U Tam'si, Evelyn Waugh, and Kateb Yacine to name a few, Waberi succeeds in bringing his country into being on "planet literature" by inserting it into a context that reaches well beyond the Horn.[9]

If Waberi finds that having to "go off and be a nomad" elsewhere in order to be a spokesman for his country is paradoxical, perhaps equally so is the fact that while his novels and short stories were written "elsewhere," they nevertheless maintain Djibouti as their primary topic. Indeed, because of war and famine in the Horn, exile and emigration have become the lot of large numbers of Somalis, whether from Djibouti or Somalia. The title of Nuruddin Farah's book about Somalis living in exile abroad, *Yesterday, Tomorrow: Voices from the Somali Diaspora,* refers to the psychological difficulty of living in the present for so many who left their countries as refugees. In *The Land without Shadows,* Farah's temporal terms of exile find their equivalents in the spatial expressions used to divide the work into its two sections, "Detour: Pages Torn from the Novel of the Imagination," and "Return: Pages Torn from the Land without Shadows."

There is no clear separation of the stories into time periods. Only five of the first eight stories are set in precolonial or colonial times ("The Primal Ogress," "The Troglodyte Root," "The Dasbiou Mystery," "The Coryphaeus of the Colony," "A Ferrous Tale"), while in the second section, only "Brazier in the Sky" is set in what seems to be a more distant past. Rather, stories about the precolonial and colonial past are juxtaposed with stories set in the postcolonial present. And while the spatial indices "Detour" and "Return" call to mind the peregrinations of nomads, many of Waberi's nomads are sedentarized or dispossessed, for eight of the nine stories in the second section deal with civil war and famine in the postcolonial era.[10] Indeed, the pages "torn from the novel of the imagination" apparently entitled *The Land without Shadows* are suggestive of such violent events. These torn pages further suggest that while there may be a lengthy linear novel somewhere that could tell the entire history of Djibouti from a single point of view, such a project is currently impossible, and even undesirable. Indeed, in the essay entitled "Comment j'ai écrit mes livres et autres considérations sommaires," Waberi compares the imagination, "that madwoman in the attic," to a "way of knowing" that follows its own logic. "Placed end to end, all of my works form a puzzle that draws its own coherence from within its textual system and from the context in which I was born. A puzzle that I am not given to read, interpret, and elucidate until afterward" (936).

In a short story from the present collection entitled "Intimate and Colossal Fragments," the narrator provides clues to this literary philosophy. "We will begin by making ours the art of the fragment because life is too complex to be seized in its entirety," declares the narrator. "By parasitizing, cannibalizing official discourses, be they by experts or from the media, by dispensing them *in naturabilus*. By reducing them to percussive echoes. . . ." (85–86). In reading, interpreting, and elucidating *The Land without Shadows*, it is clear that the art of the fragment is related to the aesthetics of the puzzle, for both require that fragments (or puzzle pieces) be assembled in order to form an image. By juxtaposing the present with the past, the individual with the collective, the colonized with the colonizer, the local with the global, *The Land without Shadows* composes an image of Djibouti that is kaleidoscopic, even cinematographic, for the "art of the fragment" offers partial but brilliantly illuminated scenes of the Djiboutian urban and rural landscape, its people and its history, as though through a camera lens.

The processes of "parasitization," "cannibalization," and "echoing" also allow for the introduction of multiple discourses, which Waberi often ironizes, whether these discourses be from outsiders or from Djiboutians themselves. Perhaps the most famous of the "outsiders" echoed in Waberi's work is the poet Arthur Rimbaud. When asked about the frequent references to Rimbaud in his work, Waberi replied, "It is not the poet Rimbaud who interests me. . . . It is as a 'gimmick' that he interests me . . . as a postmodern sign. It's like a poster of Bob Marley that someone would hang on a wall. It is as simple as that" ("Comment faire exister" 146).

In "The Seascape Painter and the Wind Drinker," Waberi alludes to Rimbaud's famous declaration, "Je est un autre" ("I is another"). But where Rimbaud "quested after an 'I' that was at once Self and Other," Waberi's characters "seek an 'I' in the undifferentiated 'We'" (41). In another reference to "the fellow from the Ardennes," Waberi's characters mention Rimbaud's *Season in Hell,* where the poet portrays himself as a *nègre,* although the work was written well before Rimbaud's adventures in East Africa. However, because they themselves have seen "a parade of a thousand infernal seasons," they decide to "forget about . . . Rimbaud," even as they remark that the poet "would roll over in his grave if he saw what's happening on our country's doorstep" (42). In "*Nabsi,*" the narrator once again alludes to Rimbaud when he compares life to "a drunken boat in the hands of the macoute general" (80). Here, the narrator alludes to Rimbaud's poem "Le Bateau ivre" ("The Drunken Boat"). However, this sign of what Rimbaud considered a necessary "disordering of the senses" in the quest for a superior poetic reality becomes for Waberi a symbol of the negative insanity created by Somali dictator General Siad Barre. While allusion to Rimbaud may be a "gimmick," Waberi's frequent references to his work nevertheless initiate a dialogue between the past and the present and introduce what he above termed a "native gaze" into discourses concerning the current state of affairs in the Horn. Finally, the frequent references to the French poet also establish Rimbaud as a model, whether postmodern or not. Waberi's prose is indeed "poetic," with its erudite vocabulary, frequent use of metaphor, alliteration (the repetition of initial consonant sounds), assonance (repetition of vowels), and predilection for puns.

Although he may play the dual role of spokesman and chronicler of the nation, Abdourahman A. Waberi is not uncritical of his people and its government. His relationship to them, he explains, is one of familiarity: "I am more familiar with immediate history as it is made by my own people. I write this national chronicle next to them, at the same time as they do, against them, and/or with them" ("Comment j'ai écrit" 934). The first short story in the present collection, "The Gallery of the Insane," is a perfect example of this "immediate history," written both "with" and "against" Waberi's compatriots. Here, the narrator takes on the Djiboutian addiction to khat chewing. Khat, or chat (*Catha edulis*), is cultivated in East Africa and the Middle East for its buds and leaves and is such a habit-forming stimulant that, as the narrator would have it, nobody can live without it: "Without khat, no life! . . . Khat is the poison and its antidote." It also incapacitates the entire city of Djibouti from "one o'clock in the afternoon to eight o'clock in the evening," so that even when lethal fires break out, the firemen, themselves in a state of lethargy, never appear (8). "The Troglodyte Root" and "The Ruminants of Routine" also take up this addiction, termed a "perpetual incarceration" in "Gallery." However, whereas in "Gallery" the narrator uses ironic humor to criticize addiction to "the malefic plant," in "The Troglodyte Root" and "The Ruminants of Routine" he is more severe. In "The Troglodyte Root," the Djiboutians have become "Troglodytes," cave dwellers who "live in slow motion" and "rarely see the light of day" because they are addicted to "a succulent root that they suck on all day long" (20, 21). In "The Ruminants of Routine," the khat chewers, or "ruminants," do everything "as a group and in haste." They are like ants, "minus . . . the taste for work" (63).

Other stories trace the history of Djibouti as a means of understanding its difficult present. For example, the solitary narrator of "The Primal Ogress" recalls the defeat ("Jab") of the ogress Bouti, the "patron saint" of Djibouti, whose heirs have "long since swamped the country in the quicksands of desperation," for they no longer follow the Xeer, the social contract that Somali pastoralists once used to govern themselves. "Ever since the death of the cannibal god-mother," says the narrator, "the trampoline of history has relentlessly shaken this indigent region" (17). A similar image of history reappears in "A Ferrous

INTRODUCTION

Tale," a story about the construction of the Franco-Ethiopian railway between 1897 and 1917. According to the narrator, the train is another effect of "the trampoline of history," for it "transformed the notion of time and space, the direction of history" (47).

While the "perfidious" tracks, "Conceived and Built by Great French Genius" are tragically compared to "two parallel lines of blood," in "A Ferrous Tale" (44, 43), French colonialism in the region is treated with humor in "The Coryphaeus of the Colony" and "The Dasbiou Mystery." "The Coryphaeus of the Colony" ridicules an ambitious but uneducated French colonist who hopes to raise a statue to himself in his village in France. "The Dasbiou Mystery" playfully alludes to the fact that before its independence in 1977, Djibouti was a Territoire d'Outre-Mer (TOM), an Overseas French Territory grouped for administrative purposes with the other French Départementes et Territoires d'Outre-Mer (DOM-TOM), the Overseas Territories and Departments of Martinique, Guadeloupe, Guyana, Réunion, New Caledonia, St. Pierre and Miquelon, and Tahiti. In "The Dasbiou Mystery," the arbitrary grouping of these countries into French possessions is emphasized when an Issa nomad comes down with a strange affliction: unable to speak his native Somali, he speaks only Creole. It isn't until Creole speakers from Martinique, Guyana, Reunion, Guadeloupe, and Haiti temporarily residing in the capital are summoned to the village that Jilaal's new language is deciphered. While the villagers explain this strange event as coincident with the construction of the Franco-Ethiopian railway, Jilaal's linguistic affliction can also be read as a metaphor for the impact of the colonial enterprise, which transplants and merges languages, peoples, and cultures and ushers in the so-called era of modernity.

The question of language is further raised in "The Seascape Painter and the Wind Drinker" as well as in "Sound Mix." As one of the characters in "The Seascape Painter and the Wind Drinker" sarcastically remarks when his companion starts speaking "like some old book published with the support of the ACCT or Edicef [development agencies of the French government]," the country has "endowed itself with four languages: two official ones because they are foreign (French for distinction and Arabic for cash from the Persian Gulf) and two national ones because they are indigenous" (40). These two national languages are of course Somali and Afar. On the other hand, in "Sound Mix," after government "officials . . . have fled with . . . the coffers of the State," and after friends and family members have followed to become refugees abroad, those who are left behind become batlike "nyctalopic zombies" who are kept alive by strange new words that come to them over the telephone wires: "Canada-United States-Australia-America-Europe-Holland-Switzerland-Scandinavia-USA" (64). While these words are as deadly as the railway tracks that "cut across" the land in "A Ferrous Tale," like the Bedouin who finally adopted the train for their own ends, those left behind end up appropriating the words as "virgin territory, a new world," in spite of the narrator's derisory comments, "What wealth! What an appropriation!" (67).

"A Woman and a Half," "Brazier in the Sky," and "Filthy Askar" are portraits of individuals and their communities. Marwo, the beautiful "woman and a half," flees the urban shantytown where her father wishes to marry her off to an old man, and seeks out her wise uncle who lives in the bush. In just a few short pages, the narrator paints the miserable slum inhabited by "fractured beings," sedentarized nomads "for whom the attraction of the city was as to a precious gem" (54), non-sedentarized nomads for whom the camel "is everything," and an explanation for the oppression of women whose "orifices" have been sewn shut since the time of the pre-Islamic Somali god WAAQ.[11] While "A Woman and a Half" tells how Marwo is vulnerable to being captured and returned to her father by a cameleer "convinced . . . of his rights as a male" (53), "Brazier in the Sky" is a portrait of Bogoreh, an impatient young nomad who must prove his manhood by capturing a young virgin from her family's encampment. However, whereas Marwo's tale is set in the contemporary period, Bogoreh's adventure takes place "when the railway had not yet made its appearance" and "God had not yet become this Cerberus that threatens men" (58). Nevertheless, the proverb uttered by Bogoreh's father at the closing of the tale is, as the narrator attests, still uttered today: "A dead man is not worth the sandals on his feet." In contrast to this enduring sentiment, "Filthy Askar" is a kind of eulogy for a tramp who was hit by a truck in the populous Samalah neighborhood of the capital. At the same time, it is a gently humoristic portrait of an impoverished community whose members band together to celebrate its native son. Filthy Askar was a real person, the author tells us, whose life experiences parallel the country's trajectory from being a French colony to becoming an independent state. Familiar with French literature, educated in Europe, a militant for independence, Filthy Askar sinks into insanity at the end of his life. "Askar is the double that we hate because we are scared to death of becoming like him. . . . I know what I'm saying, since I took the same route," says the narrator (72).

In order to make sense of this statement, it is helpful to review the use of the term "insanity" in *The Land without Shadows.* In "Gallery of the Insane," Waberi presents a typology of the madmen and -women who inhabit Djibouti. Among the mad are the former nationalists who fought for independence from the French and who "no longer understand anything at all. . . . [W]e know that France left after Giscard, but since, it's been the great black abyss. Those who govern us have gone beyond the limits of our own insanity. . . . (13)." While Askar could belong to this category, Waberi's poetic persona, the narrator who says "I" in "Filthy Askar" and in a number of other stories, could be categorized as belonging to the final category of "madmen" in "Gallery," "the reasoning madmen," who "with bravery and bravado . . . defy the most respected figures of the nation, that is, the Prophet and the President of the Republic" (15). These "noble madmen" are poets who reward "the virtuous" and punish "the malevolent, the vain, the oppressors, the disloyal, the thieves, the cheats, the overly ambitious, and, last but not least, the tribalists" (16).

While Dante Alighieri's *Inferno* with its rings of hell is a frequent reference in *The Land without Shadows*—the railroad traces "one of Dante's rings" (44) in "A Ferrous Tale" and the artists in "The Seascape Painter and the Wind Drinker" invoke Dante in reference to the civil war—the supposedly mad "champions of alliterative and elliptic Somali poetry" (15) are modeled by the likes of Sayyid Mohamed Abdille Hassan. Mentioned briefly in "Filthy Askar," Sayyid Mohamed, whom the British nicknamed "The Mad Mullah," was a Somali nationalist and poet who fought against the British in the early twentieth century with arms and with traditional Somali poetry, or *gabay*.[12] As a chronicler and spokesman of the nation who writes both "with" and "against" his people, Waberi's poetic persona continues this Somali poetic tradition.

Just as traditional Somali poets do not shy away from criticizing national and international affairs, neither do the narrators of "Braised Bodies," "A Faint Hope," "Vortex," "*Nabsi,*" and "Intimate and Colossal Fragments." Indeed, this group of stories is dedicated to governmental politics, civil war, and the American "Operation Restore Hope." "Braised Bodies" portrays a handsome young couple with political aspirations whose interest in one another outweighs their political effectiveness. Indeed, they never mention "the latest news," which the narrator then enumerates in their stead:

> . . . the wells poisoned everywhere, the necrosis of the state, the corridors of torture, the scars upon the earth, the sistrum of death, a fringe of the population in royalist insurrection, the unruly children of frantic polygamy sinking into the quagmire of political powder kegs . . . the nostalgia of nomads whose space has been confiscated . . . and the ossuary of recent history such as the Ogaden war, the refugees from Ethiopia, from Eritrea, from mutilated Somalia . . . (25)

"A Faint Hope," "Vortex," and "Intimate and Colossal Fragments" all engage elements of this "news" by juxtaposing published newspaper reports about civil war in Djibouti and famine and civil war in Somalia with reflections on these incidents by the narrator or some other "mad" character. "*Nabsi*" uses the same technique but cites "Harvest of Hate" by the Nigerian Nobel laureate Wole Soyinka in an overt comparison of events in Somalia with those in the Nigeria-Biafra civil war.[13] In "A Faint Hope," the narrator converses with the "neighborhood idiot," who recounts a brief popular uprising against the Djiboutian government. In "Vortex," the narrator contrasts fragments of published news reports about the outbreak of civil war and famine in Somalia with the individual efforts of one young Somali man to help the dying. "Intimate and Colossal Fragments" contrasts the brutality of former Somali dictator Major General Mohamed Siad Barre with the disastrous outcome of "Operation Restore Hope."[14] In this story, which closes the volume, the narrator declares before dying that "the unreality of the insane is the certainty of tomorrow" (85).

The invocation of insanity at the close of the volume not only refers readers back to the opening story of the volume but also reminds them that the task of the poet as "noble madman" is to be a "teller of some truths" (15). The narrator of the novel *Balbala* is more explicit on this topic:

> [T]he madman of the poor countries is similar to the *honnête homme* of the European Enlightenment. The mad man . . . is feared by the powerful mob. . . [for he is] able to face the dream police . . . one is not dead as long as . . . one's inheritance is safe. How to keep that part safe, how to stay alive, that is the essential question. (22)

For Waberi, the answer lies in the process of accounting for the past while casting a critical eye on the present. In *The Land without Shadows* he shows that while colonialism and imperialism have played a role in the difficult present of what he calls "this disinherited Horn" (*Balbala* 22), the inhabitants of the region have "loaded it down even more; we have added to its weight day after day without even noticing. . . ." (ibid.). Thus it is the Djiboutians who must answer the question posed by the spokesman-chronicler of the nation: "What have we been doing these past twenty years?" ("Comment j'ai écrit" 934).[15] It is the poet's proposed answer to that question that produces "a palimpsest, an addendum, a preface to our national history as it unfurls before our very eyes, whether [these eyes] be surprised or chagrined" (ibid.). Indeed, whether as palimpsest, addendum, preface, or fragment, *The Land without Shadows* puts Djibouti on the literary map.

Notes

1. Waberi, *Les Nomades,* 14. All translations in this volume, including the epigraphs to the short stories, are my own, unless otherwise noted.

2. In a number of texts from the colonial period, the Afar are also referred to as the Danakil.

3. In "Nomad's Land," I analyze in detail the ways in which Waberi engages clichés of Djibouti as "hell" as seen in works by Romain Gary, Célestin Monga, Arthur Rimbaud, and Pierre Loti, and compare them to what Waberi himself writes about his country.

4. *Les Nomades,* 44.

5. "Francophone" is here defined as someone who uses French as his or her language of communication but who is not necessarily French. Other francophone writers from Djibouti include Ali Coubba, *L'Aleph-Ba-Ta* (Paris: L'Harmattan, 1998), Idriss Youssouf Elmi, *La galaxie de l'absurde* (Paris: L'Harmattan, 1997), and Daher Ahmed Farah, *Splendeur éphémère* (Paris: L'Harmattan, 1993).

6. Although Mr. Waberi does not discuss his own writing in this essay, he shares these characteristics, except that Djibouti gained its independence in 1977.

7. See Garane, "Comment faire exister son pays sur 'la planète littérature.'" This forthcoming interview with Waberi is hereafter cited in the text as "Comment faire exister."

8. The incident was chronicled by Mark Bowden in his 1999 book *Black Hawk Down,* and later in the 2001 movie by the same name, directed by Ridley Scott.

9. Waberi's work is now being read by an international audience. *Le Pays sans ombre* and *Cahier nomade* were translated into German by Brigitte Kautz under the title *Die Legende von der Nomadensonne* (Munich: Marino Verlag, 1998). "The Gallery of the Insane," the opening story of *The Land without Shadows,* has appeared in various

INTRODUCTION

English-language anthologies, including *Xcités, the Flamingo Book of New French Writing*, trans. J. Michael Dash (London: Harper Collins, 1999); *Tenderfoots* (Johannesburg: Mail and Guardian, 2001); and, under the title "The Fools' Gallery," *Fools, Thieves & Other Dreamers, Stories from Francophone Africa* (Harare: Weaver Press, 2001). The same story was also translated into Serbian under the title "Galerija ludaka" in *Od Haitija do Madagaskara, anthologija frankofone price*, ed. Vesna Cakeljic (Belgrade: Clio, 1997). Other stories from *The Land without Shadows* have appeared in various anthologies and reviews, such as *Revue Noire*, no. 4 (1992); *The Picador Book of African Short Stories*, ed. Stephen Gray (London: Picador, 2000); *From Africa: New Francophone Stories*, ed. Adèle King (Omaha: University of Nebraska Press, 2004); and *Grand Street* 72 (2004): 71–75. *Moisson de crânes (Mietitura di Teste, Pagine per il Ruanda)* and *Balbala* appeared in Italian translations by Marie-José Hoyet in 2003 and 2004 (Rome: Editioni Lavoro).

10. In *L'Oeil nomade* (The nomadic eye), Waberi argues that, despite the ongoing processes of sedentarization, it is the nomads who can feed the country with the camels they herd for both food and trade, as well as "feed" the country's hunger for an appropriate identity. I investigate this argument in my "Nomad's Land."

11. The "sewing" of female orifices is a reference to the traditional practice of female genital excision and infibulation, whereby the clitoris, labia minora, and labia majora are removed and the vaginal opening is stitched up, leaving only a small opening.

12. Sayyid Mohamed's poetry is still popular today. Traditional Somali poets record recitations of his verses, which are then distributed on cassette tapes for purchase. See B. W. and Sheila Andrezejewski's *Anthology of Somali Poetry* for English-language translations of Sayyid Mohamed's poetry.

13. In the Nigeria-Biafra civil war (1967–70) more than one million people died of severe malnutrition.

14. Overthrown in 1991, Major General Mohammed Siad Barre fled Somalia in 1992 after ruling the country for over twenty years. He died in Lagos, Nigeria, in January 1995.

15. The period of twenty years is the approximate amount of time passed since Djiboutian independence in 1977.

BIBLIOGRAPHY

Literary Works by Abdourahman A. Waberi

Balbala. Paris: Le Serpent à Plumes, 1997; Paris: Gallimard, 2002.

Bouh et la vache magique (children's book). Illustrated by Pascale Bougeault. Vanves: Edicef, 2002.

Cahier nomade. Paris: Le Serpent à Plumes, 1996, 1999, 2002.

Moisson de crânes. Paris: Le Serpent à Plumes, 2000, 2004.

Les Nomades, mes frères, vont boire à la Grande Ourse. 1991–1998 (poèmes). Sarreguemines: Editions Pierron, 2000.

L'Oeil nomade. Djibouti: Centre Culturel Français Arthur Rimbaud, 1997.

Le Pays sans ombre. Paris: Le Serpent à Plumes, 1994, 1997, 2000, and 2002.

Rift, routes, rails (variations romanesques). Paris: Gallimard, 2001.

Transit. Paris: Gallimard, 2003.

Related Critical Works

Ahmed, Ali Jimale. *Daybreak Is Near: Literature, Class and the Nation-State in Somalia.* Lawrenceville, NJ: Red Sea Press, 1996.

Andrejewski, B. W., and Sheila Andrejewski, eds. *An Anthology of Somali Poetry.* Bloomington: Indiana University Press, 1993.

Borer, Alain. *Rimbaud en Abyssinie.* Paris: Seuil, 1984.

Bowden, Mark. *Black Hawk Down: A Story of Modern War.* New York: Atlantic Monthly Press, 1999.

Chanda, Tirthankar. "Abdourahman A. Waberi: Une oeuvre cohérente et singulière." *Notre Librairie* 146 (2001): 54–56.

Doresse, Jean. *Histoire sommaire de la Corne orientale d'Afrique.* Paris: Librairie Orientaliste Paul Geuthner, 1983.

BIBLIOGRAPHY

Farah, Nuruddin. *Yesterday, Tomorrow: Voices from the Somali Diaspora*. London and New York: Cassell, 2000.

Garane, Jeanne. "Comment faire exister son pays sur 'la planète littérature:' Entretien avec Abdourahman Waberi." In *Discursive Geographies: Writing Space and Place in French/Géographies discursives: L'écriture de l'espace et du lieu en langue française*, edited by Jeanne Garane, 133–99. Amsterdam: Editions Rodopi, forthcoming 2005.

———. "Nomad's Land: Abdourahman Waberi's Djibouti." *Renaissance noire/Black Renaissance* Summer (2003): 105–16.

Gary, Romain. *Trésors de la mer rouge*. Paris: Gallimard, 1971.

Guillebaud, Jean-Claude. "Voix rebelles de Djibouti." *Le Monde diplomatique*, January 1998, 30, http://www.monde-diplomatique.fr/1998/01/GUILLEBAUD/9767 (accessed July 2004).

Loti, Pierre. "Obock, for a Day." In *From Lands of Exile*, translated by Clara Bell. New York: William S. Gottsberger, 1888.

———. *Propos d'exile*. Paris: Calmann Lévy, 1892.

Nizan, Paul. *Aden Arabie*. Paris: Maspéro, 1960. Translated by Joan Pinkham as *Aden, Arabie* (New York: Monthly Review Press, 1968).

Oberlé, Philippe, and Pierre Hugot. *Histoire de Djibouti. Des origines à la république*. Paris: Présence Africaine, 1985.

Rimbaud, Arthur. *Oeuvres complètes*. Paris: Gallimard, 1963.

Waberi, Abdourahman A. "Comment j'ai écrit mes livres (et autres considerations sommaires)." *Modern Language Notes* 118, no. 4 (2003): 933–37.

———. "Les Enfants de la postcolonie. Esquisse d'une nouvelle génération d'écrivains francophones d'Afrique noire." *Notre Librairie* 135 (1998): 8–15.

THE LAND WITHOUT SHADOWS

To Nuruddin Farah and Tierno Monénembo,
two writers who witnessed the death of the country
of their imagination.

For Florence and for my two families from
Djibouti and Vendée.

I

DETOUR

PAGES TORN FROM

THE NOVEL OF THE IMAGINATION

THE GALLERY OF THE INSANE

Hell is empty and all of the devils are here!
—Shakespeare

It's nobody's fault.
—Evelyn Waugh

A sky so blue it is almost white. A Djibouti neighborhood in the lower city. A wooden house, like all the others, with an aluminum roof. Here and there on the dirty hole-ridden roof—warped by rust (humidity reigns supreme) as much as by wear—the most unlikely objects jostle each other and resonate with strange echoes: a ball, deflated and shrunken by the heat, a deformed old bicycle wheel, a tattered straw hat, a shabby shoe, a rag, a few pitiful nails.

In a shaded corner of the veranda, leaning against the partition, a man—older rather than younger—is seated on the raffia mat. In front of him, there is a low, wobbly little table on which, one next to the other, have been placed a little red cooler to keep the water fresh, a thermos for the hot and heavily spiced tea (cinnamon, cloves, cardamom, and ginger), a glass, and a cup. Wrapped in an often wetted rag, just under the spigot of the cooler: khat, the object of everyone's desire in this part of the world. The magic plant. The malefic plant. Khat comes in bundles of twigs held together by a cork-colored fiber from a banana leaf.

This man with the half-closed eyes of those who have stayed up all night: he's my father. Awaleh ruminates, as we say here with a note of pride. To tell the truth, he does not ruminate—he chews his khat as one chews tobacco. Or as one chews gum. And about every fifteen minutes, he takes a swallow of cold water, then of hot tea. Khat makes you thirsty. Khat makes your legs tingle. My father changes position every half hour: after the right side (his favorite), he shifts to his left side. He always proceeds in the same way. Always. Khat punctuates the lives of the people in this blasted country. Without khat, no life! From one o'clock in the afternoon to eight o'clock in the evening, khat keeps men (and women) alive. Without it, what to do, how to live? For some, only the voice of the muezzin breaks into this well-established ritual.

In a world adrift, men latch on to the most fragile thing: the twigs of an Ethiopian bush. This plant hardens them in return. Khat is the poison and its antidote—in other words, a perpetual incarceration.

The most lethal fires always break out during the afternoon, when, in a state of lethargy, men and women, children and animals aspire to daydreaming. A few muddy streets farther on, a little house is being consumed by fire. Like messiahs, the firemen keep people waiting. As usual. Maybe they will never come. No matter. It is said that they no longer know which way to head. Last week, a ninety-year-old neuropath perished, exhausted and suffocated under the rubble. A handful of ashes seemed to indicate all that was left of the old lady when the fire was overcome by the impassive neighborhood.

Fire, that malicious Prometheus, arrogantly chews on the work of city planners. In full sight of everyone, fire labors in its lunatic dance, tracing zigzagging alleys in the lower city, taking with it everything in its path like some Acheron, leaving only a few rough, stunted posts the color of anthracite.

More recently, a high-level city planner gave this very speech to some helpless victims:

"Fire gives no gifts, but you must agree that the only fires that break out are the ones we deserve. Note that we never deplore damage caused by some pyromaniac in the real city."

In this part of town, fire has free reign.

THE GALLERY OF THE INSANE

As hesitant as a frail skiff, life springs from the empty belly of a little girl; this girl-child with the very emaciated face feeds a child just as sickly. Which is the mother? Which is the off-spring?

Meanwhile, not far from there, my father is seated on a raf-fia mat. Leaning against the partition as is his habit, he chews mechanically. Outside, there is a ruckus. The hot wind stiffens faces so they look like unfeeling masks. Streets are emptied of their passersby; life slows down, becomes more fluid. There will no longer be anyone in the streets. The din will have disap-peared. The phantom hour stealthily approaches. Khat grips the city with its power. While waiting for zombification, noth-ing else matters. The outside world has ceased to exist. It is the phantom hour.

In alleys dusty because never paved, piled with offal, allu-vium, and coproliths, a few women squawk at their thresholds. The one across the street shouts,

"Dirty brat born of the Devil's water, go get a nice cold Coca-Cola for that absent father of yours! Do you hear me, you know very well that khat dries his throat. Come over here you little bastard!"

Her neighbor chimes in with a quavering voice, as if to give substance to her story:

"My husband is exactly the same way. Without Coca-Cola, khat would come out of his behind like a refugee baby with a vicious case of diarrhea." This woman, an aide in the neigh-borhood dispensary, likes to impress the neighbors by using new terms systematically borrowed from the hospital milieu. In turn, a third, a tall black woman whose breasts, flattened against her thorax, can easily be glimpsed through the trans-parent *diric*,* proclaims,

"Mine is like a child. I have never seen an adult who likes sweet things so much. Three Coca-Colas and tea full of sug-

*A very transparent and light dress worn a bit like a sari.

ar every day. Sometimes, I wonder whether his crazy mother didn't suckle him with Coca-Cola."

From a back courtyard, the monotonous voice of Saïd Hamarghod, the most prolix singer in the Somali language, harps on this melancholy refrain:

" . . . I do not lament
I was born for pain
One day I will be healed
One day I will be healed . . ."

My father ruminates in his corner. Regular visitors, cousins, near or distant relatives, tribal affiliates, and various acquaintances rival each other to come close to him. They come to see him, one in order to chew with him, another to borrow a bundle of khat that will never be paid for. Each has found a little spot for his skinny behind. At two o'clock, everyone is just about ready. The khat session has already started. Outside, it's the phantom hour.

Hamoud, the blacksmith, remains one of the most unassuming personalities in the neighborhood. Nevertheless, his peers recognize his incredible dexterity unmatched especially in the poor part of town. True to his reputation, at the suicide hour, the moment when the sun's rays are sharper than glass shards, Hamoud arrives at his workplace: a pile of metal that serves as his outdoor workshop. For history with a small "h" (which often illuminates history with a capital "H"), Hamoud is a Toumal. That is to say that he belongs to a caste judged to be inferior and, thus, shunned by all the Somali ethnic groups. Because they work with iron, the Toumal are the victims of veritable but unacknowledged segregation. In our neighborhood, the gossips claim that Hamoud rashly gives himself over to the Devil's brew. Others solemnly swear by their late great-grandfather, who died following the Great Drought called the "Devastator," that Hamoud hides his liter of wine in a flask

THE GALLERY OF THE INSANE

of cough syrup slipped under his iron bed. Among the black-smith's adversaries there are a good number of mosque faith-ful led by the neighborhood chief, Haji War Amoussa. In an indescribable fit of anger, War Amoussa almost gouged out the eye of Hamoud's apprentice, a scrawny blacksmith-mechanic whose precise age one would hesitate to guess at. Halloul did not try to press charges because he knows full well that War Amoussa is untouchable. People whisper that an old domestic dispute partly explains the relentless hatred War Amoussa feels for Hamoud.

At one end of an alley full of ruts, two lycée students of un-usual maturity converse brilliantly (since there is no university in this country, one is called an intellectual as soon as one sets foot in the lycée).

The first says to the second:

"Our country is a grandiose inferno that Antonin Artaud would not have disowned."

The other retorts using the same grave tone:

"With Independence and afterward, we got nothing, not even an enlightened demagogue who would speak rivers on which to carry us away, who might speak to us of national uprisings, in short, who would soothe us with illusions—how frustrating . . ."

Bob Marley was singing "Waiting in Vain" in another little street.

At three in the afternoon, the first signs—preludes to the *mirghan** (Solomon's hour, following the expression of a Yemeni poet and khat lover who knows what he is talking about)—appear in broad daylight. People get up to stretch their legs a bit. They might as well seize the opportunity to go empty their bladders over at the latrine, with its swarm of flies, its network of spiderwebs, its countless geckos, its big purple

*That particular moment when, at twilight, khat attains its most con-vulsive effect.

cockroaches, its young rats. The most alert ruminants reluctantly go to the nearby grocery store to buy the second bottle of Coca-Cola and the third pack of American cigarettes. The most voracious—they are legion—forget their pride in order to borrow one more bundle of khat, to the great dismay of their usual supplier, my father, for example. The wisest—they are rare—resolve to save a bit of money by parsimoniously chewing their skinny twigs of khat. They are the ones who throw away neither the toughest leaves nor those that are the most unrewarding under the tongue. Those leaves are usually given to the beggars and the insane who scour the neighborhood.

Every neighborhood possesses its horde of lunatics. Each lunatic suffers from his own special "lunacy" which characterizes him, each cultivates his particular art, manages his own dementia as he sees fit. Every lunatic is a separate and individual "lunacy." And some distinguish themselves by their innate charm and their own particular appeal.

There are the zealous lunatics, generally the stone throwers. Vengeful and malevolent, they initially attack children, women, drunkards—another race of lunatics in this country—and the ill, or those presumed to be such. The zealous lunatics fear the competition, insolent and disloyal in their eyes, from the armies of beggars, many of whom come from the droves of refugees expelled by governments using bludgeons and barbed wire. The zealous lunatics denounce to whoever wishes to listen the ignominious and insulting mendacity of these people coming from elsewhere, thus from nowhere. Fiercely jealous of their neighborhood (because they are the true native sons), the zealous lunatics pursue normal people and foreigners. They can prove to be murderous, for these sons born of the neighborhood recollect distant battles, those fought for Independence, among others.

"We zealous lunatics were the most ardent nationalists. We fought against the French. We left the most zealous among us on the fields of honor at La Poudrière, at Gabode or Loyada, not to mention the front lines where the enemy soldiers were more numerous than flies on an open wound. Well, shit, all of that is past, nothing but hot air . . . You want us to admit it: now, we no longer understand anything at all. Truly, we miss the time of the Kaireh Addeh,* who at least had the merit of clarity. Nevertheless, we are not fooled, we know that France left after Giscard, but since, it's been the great black abyss. Those who govern us have gone beyond the limits of our own insanity, we who are the so-called professional zealous lunatics . . ."

There are also the malicious madmen, unequaled parasites and peerless flatterers. People say that they are so by necessity, because they don't know how to do anything else. Above all others, they value women as their victims, wealthy or not, on whom they lavish advice paid for by cash on the spot. They know how to strike the sensitive chord in each woman. They are content to utter a great, demented cry (that once was considered specific to blacks alone) when faced with difficult cases.

"Women, you are the most beautiful, the most generous, the most noble: we observe that deep within you; we detect the tiniest signal hidden in the enigma of your personality. Go on, buy us some khat today, Friday, the day of our Lord and not that of Nabi Issa.** The stars couldn't be more favorable, so everything is going to turn out right for all of you! It is written in the folds of your necks and in the fleshiest parts of your inner thighs."

This delights more than one young miss awaiting a very well arranged marriage.

Contrary to the malicious madmen, there is a pack of silent lunatics. Their defining physical characteristic: copious locks like those of the followers of Saint-Haile-Selassie-of-Harar and of Saint-Tafari-of-Jamaica. Once men of wisdom and good fathers in the tradition of the herders of the Horn of Africa, it is

---

*The name that Djiboutians jokingly give the French, and by extension, to all whites. Addeh also means "clarity."
**Jesus Christ.

whispered that they have since been touched with a sort of pernicious grace. The silent lunatics allow themselves the luxury of not saying a word while continuing to scratch their heads and their backs as though, unbeknownst to the entire world, they were watching over the secrets that rule the universe in order to keep them intact. They have a look that pierces you, penetrates you, leads imbeciles to say that they have something mystical about them. Mute as Buddhas, their silences immediately make your blood run cold: they are attributed glorious pasts or amorous adventures out of the ordinary.

"Do you know why this man does not speak?" says an ordinary man pointing at a silent lunatic.

"Apparently, the day of his marriage, his ninth wife died asphyxiated like the other eight," he adds.

In any case, one thing is for certain: the silent lunatics make others talk. Consequently, this keeps them alive.

There are not only madmen, there are also madwomen in this part of the world where serious journalism has long been displaced by rumor. Among the cohort of madwomen, people cry out when faced with the gang of the exhibitionist, vulva-displaying madwomen. Their high rank always causes them to be followed by a band of urchins, many of whom are preparing for the profession of wandering lunatic, blatantly encouraged by the authorities, who no longer know what to come up with next. Thus, the madwomen-who-exhibit-their-vulvas, true queen bees that they are, never go anywhere without their swarm of drones. At rush hour, at every intersection, an exhibitionist madwoman deftly lifts her *diric* so as to display her assets. She is a hit, especially with the faithful from the mosque. From now on, the faithful no longer pretend to turn their eyes away from the representatives of Lucifer. They revel in this collection of shrunken organs with shriveled lips that stink of excrement, urine, and the froth of men in a rush not to be discovered with a notorious prominent madwoman-who-exhibits-her-vulva. In truth they make many happy, but all they get in return are hard words (a little like the Administration, cash cow of the nation).

THE GALLERY OF THE INSANE

"We are goddesses, you come to visit us often enough. Come on, when will there be a temple for us?" demands a mad-woman.

Finally, there are the noble madmen, noble in their mad-ness. Champions of alliterative and elliptic Somali poetry, they are the most high-ranking of the profession, the most feared as well. These men are dangerous. These are the reasoning madmen, speakers of a few truths and lightning rods for ce-lestial thunderbolts. They are becoming more and more rare. They are a race that is proudly headed for extinction. They throw mimosa thorns at their current enemies: for example, at any important person. With bravery and bravado, they defy the most respected figures of the nation, that is, the Prophet and the President of the Republic. When a mad teller of a few truths enters a room, everyone falls silent, some suddenly leave on tiptoe, others—for no reason at all—break into a profuse sweat; still others express the desire to vomit, feel their legs be-gin to tingle, or experience urinary incontinence. The boldest, like Haji War Amoussa, the neighborhood chief, try to corrupt him:

"Here is the Devil in person. Give him something to drink! Are you thirsty? Here, take this bundle of khat and this bill to pay for the bus to Balbala,* *Soub'han'Allah,* go, go my son . . ." And the reasoning madman repays him in kind. He rummages through the chief's past in order to unearth buried secrets, cam-ouflaged histories, falsified identities, or repressed episodes:

"Tell me, Haji, since when are you so generous, a man who not so long ago fought with vultures over offal and entrails in order to resell them at a high price on the market? And your twelfth pilgrimage, how did you pay for it? In the most dishon-est manner possible, I presume?"

The madman teller of some truths is merciless as soon as he opens his mouth. He is fond of shocking phrases and masters

*Large slum at the edge of Djibouti, where the poorest are crowded together.

a volubility and a clairvoyance rightly recognized and appreciated by all. Some see in him the moral conscience—if there is one—of the neighborhood. This lunatic knows the individual value of each person in a society that is collective and stifling for the individual, he rewards the virtuous—more and more scarce—and he punishes in his own way the malevolent, the vain, the oppressors, the disloyal, the thieves, the cheats, the overly ambitious, and, last but not least, the tribalists. That is why his enemies are more numerous than the beads on a chaplet. They always demand an exemplary deed, they repeat everywhere that he must be quartered for all his insolences, for his disregard for tradition. But the mad teller of many truths continues to hound the false bigots by revealing their weaknesses in public: this one is a homosexual, that one an inveterate alcoholic, etc.

The demystifying madman vehemently attacks the die-hard opportunists. Straightaway, the madman-who-thwarts-chaos proclaims his personal credo:

"I have nothing against suffering humanity, clairvoyant madman that I am. I hunt the bad lots. Oh! Oh! Oh! I warn you, I am a thousand years old . . ."

Leaning against the partition, my father continues to chew.

THE PRIMAL OGRESS

Grass must grow and children must die.

—Victor Hugo

First there was the ogress, the forgotten mother, the creature sprung from the swamps: a cruel, hairy creature with razor-sharp canines, long sharpened fingernails, and a coat of worn hyena skin. In one hand she carried a lance of wrought iron and in the other a pilgrim's staff. Her skin was so cracked and covered with scabs that she resembled a saurian.

There was the amphibious ogress, accomplished predator of men. Her tracks have been marked in golden letters in this region since time immemorial: she is the spirit of this disparate country, a bit like the Roman she-wolf. She is the mother who gives and takes away life, the whale from the depths of the abyss with the unfathomable belly.

In the beginning there was the ogress. Then came the men who conquered her. Her death had given birth to this moldering, leprous white city, which bears in its breast her indelible seal. Let it be understood: Djibouti (or more precisely "Jabouti"), according to a persistent legend, means the defeat (Jab) of the ogress (Bouti). The ogress is thus the nourishing mother, the patron saint of this centenary city.

Ever since the death of the cannibal godmother, the trampoline of history has relentlessly shaken this indigent region, already stricken by the murderous will of an imperial sun.

Had he dreamed his ultimate dream, he who claimed the right to imagination? There he was, as idle as an apostle might be on the day of Final Judgment. There he was, looking at the ocean (communicating with it, as those skilled in animism would say), an ocean from which he did not eat the fat tortoises, the shellfish, or even the fish. The ocean: the sole boundary of his universe. But the breeze was as dear to him as the light of day or its brilliance in his eyes.

The heirs of the ogress had long since swamped the country in the quicksands of desperation. As the sole survivor of this bitter misfortune, he gazes at the ocean day and night. Time is no longer of the slightest importance to him. Just as before the ruin, he strives to pray five to seven times a week (depending), as if a clearly rusty but functioning machine suddenly recalled its far-off movements. Back then, hope was not sold at auction; no demiurge was going to restore it! At nightfall, he lay on his back to gaze at the sky, to survey the stars. He slept in the open like the herders of yesteryear, in the era of the Xeer* and before the deluge.

He remembered that, like the ogress, he was alone on this coast, rolled up in a ball, abandoned, naked as on the day he was born. He wondered whether he had not been generated by the humus and flatulence of the ocean, if his great-great-grandmother were not the primal ogress?

"How beautiful are the stars in an unchanged sky!" he remarked each time he got ready to sleep.

And what dreams of escape, restless to say the least, what secret hopes, what relentless eyes staring at the horizon, the blue line, the ocean frontier!

"Flee, over there, flee," preached the poet. The oily waters from the boats following the coast of the country carried the scent of freedom. And what of the generous full-figured forms of popular Italian or Indian actresses on the tattered screen in the principal movie theater, overflowing as soon as night set the cover of cool shadow on the suffocating basin of this city?

All of that was well before the deluge.

In his irenic delirium he had remembered the legend of the ogress, she who gives life and takes it away again; was she not alone as he was on this indistinct shore? She had the ocean as a boundary and the sky for her only universe. The men who had conquered her had since eaten each other, like wolves. Was the she-wolf not the mother of Rome?

*The social contract that governed Somali clans.

THE PRIMAL OGRESS

He arose, a bit somber, looked at the black sky scattered with uniformly twinkling crystals, and before going to sleep glanced for the last time at the ocean which no longer had the strength to push to shore the last sluggish and ungrateful waves, devoid of their foamy diadems. With resignation, they were embracing the immutable unmoving sand, itself indifferent to their awkward caresses. Taken by surprise, expelled from his hole behind a small dark rock, a dazed crab teetered under the assault of the lascivious waves. The night swallowed him up.

From the time of the Ancients it was said that God, in a day of anger, had ordered the ocean never to go beyond its natural limits so as not to distress men.

First there was the ogress, the beast sprung from the Gate of Tears (Bab-el-Mandeb);* there was the redeeming word against the triumph of forgetfulness, the breadth of silence.

From the Greeks who visited this region several centuries ago up to the dictatorships of today's sand-covered republics, condottieres and other crowned heads had been bent either on immuring people into the most obsessive silence or on conveniently removing their gags, but in order to subsequently take hostage their passions and their most commonly shared desires. But had he himself not kept the memory of those days of gloom, outrage, and mourning alive? Was the past too truncated to emerge from the archives of his memory? Why this silence?

He was sailing the ocean seated on a lily pad. Aden is across the way, but it is not Eden either. He was sailing . . . The ogress had passed this way: ever since, everything is famine and anarchy, war and division.

---

*Literally, Gate of Tears; a strait joining the Red Sea and the Gulf of Aden, between Yemen and the north of the Republic of Djibouti.

THE TROGLODYTE ROOT

Between the Sinai Peninsula and the Island of Socotra,
you have to accept an environment in which men are
truly foreign: they can do nothing, their wishes,
their desires do not shake the permanence of the desert.
—Paul Nizan, *Aden, Arabie*

A foreign traveler arrives in the land of the Troglodytes, a strange people. He exhibits his talents as a public entertainer. He is not averse to immersing himself in the affairs of the town, which gets along one year at a time. He is a proselyte to politics, is persnickety about protocol, a claustrophobic tribune who has encountered many a trial and tribulation since he began haranguing crowds with his exhausting and voluble speeches.

But what does he expect? A halo of glory?

A waste of time in this land of Troglodytes. These treacherous men are bent over from slaving away in dark holes. Real bats. Veritable screech owls. These men with hardened, cracked hands vegetate in the mediocrity of a lackluster life with hopes long since dashed. Heavyhearted, they live in slow motion. Some, it seems, have rarely seen the light of day. Most of them rush to play primitive games under the topaz-colored street lights. As soon as night falls, the Troglodytes come out of their holes to get some air, lurk in dives and greasy spoons from another era where a sad singer intones a languorous lament. Their eyes are accustomed neither to the harsh light of the imposing sun nor to the glaring truth. Therefore, they hate orators, loudspeakers, and garrulous old women. Therefore they vehemently reject indoor games, political gatherings, and palavers in the bush. In short, for the Troglodytes, to vegetate is to live, and light is synonymous with death. In the beginning there was the insidious silence that favored servility and deafness during two hundred years of colonization.

The Troglodytes systematically destroy termite mounds in order to feed on the insects; besides, they abhor the pointed, conical, phallic forms of the mounds, which they find insulting, and which do not fail to call to mind some of their detested totems, rather resembling the sculptures of Easter Island.

Fagou means "bad god" in their language, but also "termite hill" and "trash heap." On the other hand, *fabou* could be translated, not without some hesitation, as "divine goodness," "gaping hole," "minstrel," or again as "absolute ecstasy." All of this appears on their secular calendar. In the Troglodyte firmament, *fagou* and *fabou* eternally coexist, attacking each other every twenty days (a cycle that is as much religious as it is political and social) and *fagou* always gets the upper hand over its alter ego. Then follow long silences, ruminations, betrayals, and sacrifices, necessary for observing the end of the cycle. Every good Troglodyte molts, which is to say, after every cycle he will change political opinion, relationships, profession, religion, and often even family. It is commonplace for a Troglodyte to betray his closest relatives every twenty days in order to uphold his reputation and social status. It is not rare for him to also exchange his hole, his cavity, his cave, for another hole, cavity, or cave similar in every respect to the first one, just to turn his back on those who were his friends the day before. Was it the nature of the Troglodytes to be constantly changing and unpredictable chameleons? Why such strange mores?

These oddities, this strange behavior can be attributed to their eating habits, or more precisely to a succulent root that they suck on all day long. They practice this sucking in compact groups or dispersed in the dark corners of their caves where a murderous, suffocating heat prevails. They succumbed to the delights of this root seventy years ago out of a taste for goety. A root so singular and pernicious that adults have lost the habit of fornicating, and children, instead of playing like children, have acquired the depressed look of an abandoned wife. With exemplary insolence, the Troglodytes of a neighboring nation, craftier but no less ancient, furnish these succulent roots, which earn them gigantic sums. This rather lucrative traffic grows from year to year, in complete impunity, much to the detriment of the most sagacious Troglodytes, who can see no farther than the thresholds of their caves. A few slightly ostentatious foreign Troglodytes have gotten rich trading in the sweet roots, which cause cavities in the healthy and the ill alike in this lunatic country. The trading company has acquired a legion of pimps, an army of wardens, a pack of poet-flatterers as well as a dozen fortune-tellers who read tarot cards for them every twenty days.

Because of this succulent and soporific root, and especially because of the trade in it, the Troglodytes live on bad terms with one another. They become sullen, abuse each other publicly, whine, and, most despairingly, are lacking in happy songs.

In a not-so-distant past, these Troglodytes were fierce, proud herders who rambled with their herds in search of fresh grass in the savanna. They were feared by their enemies—killing was a sport for this bellicose people. Today, they carry the tumultuous tomb of a glorious past on their shoulders. They have fallen so far that an obscure foreign schoolteacher took pride in writing their first history, entitled *Subterranean Chronicles,* as well as a little work of geography in engravings. In our time, the Troglodytes celebrate neither baptisms, birthdays, deaths, nor marriages. Their memory is fossilized, their history petrified:

"A people with neither head nor tail is like a succulent plant with no roots," says one of their proverbs that has since fallen into disuse.

Young Troglodytes imitate their elders, who only marry their cousins or the daughters of their close friends, who are often their cousins.

Onto the clans, tribes, families, and other vestiges of a very ancient ethnic organization have been grafted pressure groups, economic corporations, financial interests, and recently formed social categories. There are the nouveaux riches, the parvenus, the speculators, all greedy and arrogant. There are the former rulers, the sultans of old, presently blind and bedridden. A one-eyed minority holds power. Finally, as for the Troglodyte masses, they remain at once deaf, dumb, and blind.

To a foreign eye, like the one belonging to our traveler, it is not easy to collect data, classify, itemize, or catalog the Troglodytes on the basis of their exterior indices, for the simple reason that there are a multitude of imposters: a long line of the deaf, dumb, and blind who wish to pass as simply blind, of the blind who pretend to be blind only in one eye (like the minority in power), and of the deaf-mutes who pretend to speak. Here, all the combinations come together in broad daylight.

Moreover, the Troglodytes possess a characteristic that makes them the all-time champions of lamentation, the professionals of complaining and whining. The largest cave of the country has been baptized "The Court of Lamentations." The best-known jazz group carries the tender name of the "Nighttime Whiners." In this country old people never stop getting older, and virgins grieve because they can no longer find a suitable young Troglodyte.

In the large chambers of the caverns, the bones of rats, their principal nourishment along with the termites, pile up so as to obstruct a large part of the cavernous space. From this pile wafts a stench that would kill common mortals in our world.

But what effect can bad odors have on the Troglodytes shut away in their holes, deaf, dumb, blind, and lacking a sense of smell? Even Mother Nature is annoyed at having to carry such a people in her entrails. Thus there has not been the least drop of rain for an eternity of eternities. Thus the sun has decided to rise no longer in the realm of the Troglodytes. That is why they live in the shadow of their shades. That is why they become the phantoms of their phantoms.

BRAISED BODIES

Truth is body.

—Nuruddin Farah, *Maps*

Molten words, scattered embers, diorites expelled from gaping lips, firebrand caresses, when brutal, leaden, muteness crumbles and the body seeks its voice like a plaice returning to its estuary.

—Assia Djebar, *Fantasia: An Algerian Cavalcade*

He. She. She in him. He talks and talks. He and she face the crowd. She concentrates intensely, quivers and shimmers. A time for suspicion? . . . We wait to hear what she will say to us. She complies, accuses the whole world, begins again, and excuses the country's rather ineffectual political officials.

He. She. He in her. How many more? Since when does the res publica meddle with the drama of couples in our country? He talks and talks, his bushy head above the lectern. A white suit and mysterious dark glasses. The quavering voice of the androgyne.

People cannot be placated with vague promises of wells to be dug in the mire of expectation. They cannot be smoked out with pious wishes for a reprieve. Come back next week, we need dynamic and motivated young graduates. His Excellency the Minister is absent. We have been living in a place of sacrifice for ages.

He. She. She in him. He talks and talks. She licks with her lips of coral. Braised bodies: what nature gives us to gaze upon with pleasure. They are agave flowers in the ecstasy of an arborescent embrace.

He whispers nearly inaudible words. She sighs deeply. A rustling of fabric—the prelude to a tender frenzy. A naked knee emerges from beneath the sheet. Moans in the bed and a gaping void in the night. A quarter moon stands guard.

He whispers, "I'm talking about the unhealed wound."

"I know, I know," she murmurs in her toothy voice.

Before the crowd he cries, "The open and putrid wound of our country is indeed tribalism!"

People stomp with impatience. He says not a word about the latest news: the mobilization intended to be extensive, the wells poisoned everywhere, the necrosis of the state, the corridors of torture, the scars on the earth, the sistrum of death, a fringe of the population in royalist insurrection, the unruly children of frantic polygamy sinking into the quagmire of political powder kegs, deaf to words of reason, and the nostalgia of nomads whose space has been confiscated, clawed destiny bearing down upon them, and the ossuary of recent history such as the Ogaden war, the refugees from Ethiopia, from Eritrea, from mutilated Somalia, and those who are called "the divided herds," and . . . Rare are the vestals in the azure of time, the gentle hissing of the soul . . .

He in she. Rump to thighs. A narrows in the night. Everything there is emptiness, pain, and desire. He is she in the immensity of the instant. Bodies tattooing the nadir in the darkened room. Cleft, the first body shaken: the skin scored through, a moment of perdition, a channel to another world, to another epidermis, a shudder down to the toes. A rose accepted, a body cleft.

A view of the sun in the land of sun. The crowd drinks in promises. Drops bead on their faces. He points a finger. Prominent citizens have succeeded in transforming the arid country—even where the colonial administration had partly failed—into an organized bordello, a makeshift bawdy house under topaz lights, and the (young) girls into delicacies for soldiers on guard duty. Wandering legionnaires sample the choice cuts in half-blind bars to the tune of a vaguely oriental fiesta as matrons look on . . . And hope incinerated from the very beginning . . . and herders headed off to search for their herds (without Kalachnikovs, if you please, yes, as in the days of old) . . . and a teacher explains to his students:

DETOUR

"A paltry opera is what I call the result of a disappointment whose sensitive nerve lies deep in education. In truth, we are raised within the clearly defined goal of one day supporting our brothers, our sisters, our parents, the extended family, and why not a part of, or even the entire clan? And yet we are unleashed in the urban jungle without a red cent, and we are (I already and you soon) condemned to repeat the paltry opera for everyone—maintaining the illusion that someday we will be useful for something or another. And on that day? What day? There is no work in the stifling marketplace, tigers prowl around the doors; take care of the infants, who are less fortunate than their elders . . . and always waiting: a hotbed of dissent isolated in a sea of ice . . . take care of the infants, Grand Guignol is on the prowl (logorrhea, wild gestures, tired pupils) . . . find a pittance, find one's niche under the sun; yes, class, there is no work, and the supposed prophylactic happiness of the single party system . . . and the country goes on, dislocated . . ."

He. She. He in she. He talks and talks in front of the sleeping crowd. She looks at him languidly. He, a young man in his prime, an Apollo with cinnabar lips. She might have escaped from a remote harem.

The former horn of plenty is nostalgic for the bacchanalia of the age before Muhammad. Hot baths and skin anointed with animal oils. Alcoves and almost incestuous pleasures performed on sheep skins. Like the restive enneads. Offers of enticing rumps, and demands for well-rounded pocketbooks. In the Bay of Abyssinia, the girls are often beautiful and Beelzebub was rousing his army. The earth was groaning beneath a nascent volcano.

He. She. He and she in a deafening embrace. If not for her voice, she could have been taken for the male, and vice versa. They are in me. They are me, the androgyne with eyes of jade and a mystic gaze.

THE DASBIOU MYSTERY

All men are born insane, some stay that way.
—Samuel Beckett

An extraordinary story is circulating throughout the land. In Dasbiou, a quiet little village and unimposing train station on the Djibouti–Addis Ababa line, the sky is always blue—it is endless summer—but the inhabitants can speak of nothing but this story. The august elders who converse serenely outside Goffané café, Place de la Gare, no longer know which saint—or *sayyid*—to invoke. The once intrepid schoolchildren of Dasbiou no longer deign to play soccer on the bare field next to the residence of the assistant commissioner with its giant euphorbia and its shimmering colors of bister, saffron, and vermilion. Matrons, usually so avid for gossip, seem to be at a loss for words. From time to time, one of them raises her arms to the sky, invoking who knows what deity. Nobody ventures to make a public pronouncement on the origin of the evil; tongues barely loosen among friends or within the family.

Rayaleh Abaneh, the elder of Dasbiou, who is not a poet, cannot get over it. It seems like a dream. It is unthinkable. What an unbelievable story! Smack in the middle of Issa territory, no, such a thing has never been seen before! Ever since the train came, strange things have been happening. Rayaleh Abaneh has decided to convene a committee of Wise Men on Friday, that is, exactly a week to the day following the incident.

"According to tradition, the forty-four greatest Wise Men must meet on the occasion of unusual occurrences. Let them come from all over the land, from between-the-two-seas,* let

*The area between the coast of the Red Sea (from Djibouti to Zeila) and the Awash river, favorite stomping grounds of the Issa.

them all come! . . . Ah, do not forget to have a word about it with his Majesty the Ogass,* may God watch over his venerable person."

For the past two days, this was how the elder Rayaleh Abaneh had been giving precise orders to his young lieutenants: Dirir the elementary schoolteacher, Saad the postal worker, and Guedid the khat dealer. As a seasoned traveler, the latter was charged with alerting the Wise Men residing in the western part of the country. He was to take the first train and would stop only in the cities or villages where one of the forty-four Wise Men lived: Aïchaa, Hadagalla, Harawa, Milleh, Chinileh, Awash, Hourso . . . Dire-Dawa, the residence of his Majesty the Ogass.

The two companions, Dirir and Saad, had their work cut out for them. Their mission was to crisscross the Republic of Djibouti and its main cities: Ali Sabieh, Dikhil, Tadjourah, Obock, Arta, Ouéah, and finally Djibouti, the capital.

Have I already mentioned that the entire country had its eyes riveted on Dasbiou, which attracted renewed attention as a result?

"Dasbiou! Dasbiou! What a pretty name!" exclaimed the citizens of the capital, to many of whom the existence of this little village, as isolated as an oasis in Arabia, was completely unknown. Just like a pebble on the moon.

On Friday as planned, the forty-four Wise Men were all present at the much-awaited rendezvous. All of them demonstrated a desire to get to the serious business at hand. Forget the formal greetings, it was imperative to get down to brass tacks! Many came by train, others by buses specially chartered for the occasion. Two or three arrived leading their caravans as in the past. Still others managed with the means at hand, that is, in an ambulatory manner. Finally, one of them, a former immigrant laborer in the Gulf states, stepped out of his private helicopter like a harried businessman. The forty-four Wise Men, or most of them, sported handsome beards dyed reddish with henna (which is no longer the prerogative of women), were

---

*The Ogass is the spiritual leader of the Issa.

well into their sixties, and could be distinguished by their inexhaustible knowledge of custom and tradition. They revered, it is said, the secular harmony between the visible world and the other world, invisible, unknown, or simply forgotten by mortals. Thus the forty-four Wise Men met the okal* of Dasbiou, the very respectful and no less wise Rayaleh Abaneh, and held counsel under the celebrated tree of Galilee, otherwise known as an acacia. Following a long, ceremonious speech enhanced by an abundance of respectful greetings required by protocol, Rayaleh Abaneh, the master of ceremonies, unveiled what had come to be called the Dasbiou mystery.

"*Alhamdoullilah!* I will begin at the beginning as required by the very holy Kitab.** Great Wise Men, open wide your ears and hold your breath, for you have never before heard such a story, you can take my word for it . . . (*silence*) . . . but it will be up to you to judge by the evidence."

Upon hearing these words, one of the Wise Men, Awaleh Absieh from Holl-Holl, I think, made the following clever remark, which has since been elevated to the rank of a proverb: "Honorable Sage," said he to Rayaleh Abaneh, "if we are all meeting under the tree of Galilee, it is because there is rarely rain without clouds."

"Yes," acquiesced the elder calmly, "if the truth be told, there is a snake in the grass." And he immediately went on: "Understand if you can: here is the story as God willed that it should happen just outside my door, right in the middle of Dasbiou and not far from the mosque . . . *Soubhan'Allah,* isn't that already a sign in itself?" he went on, raising his arms in a gesture of powerlessness.

Ears pricked up, eyes cast toward the horizon, the Wise Men are attentive to Rayaleh Abaneh, an excellent storyteller by the way.

"A young Bedouin from my clan, Jilaal Okieh, came to Dasbiou to see his brother Assoweh, said to be an upright and

*Village elder.
**Qur'an.

prominent official in the city. Up to that point, nothing out of the ordinary. Jilaal is an ordinary young man like you and me, a cameleer, a bachelor, and a man of God. His is a life of peregrination following a herd of dromedaries, a life of deprivation, but also a life of poetry and liberty . . ." Rayaleh Abaneh cleared his throat and went on:

"Jilaal is a brave cameleer, a valorous warrior happy to live the life of an ascetic just as our ancestors did . . ." He paused, pretended to be at a loss for words, and after a short interval stated with gusto:

"Only, as soon as he set foot in our quiet city, he was no longer the same. Jilaal was bewitched by a jinni. Believe me, he exhibited the same symptoms as Aïdid Sanbour, the one who suffocated to death. No sooner had he begun to look for his brother than he showed signs of fatigue, of irritation. Signs of suffocation as well. He told himself that he could sleep, if only a wink, under the old laurel in front of the train station. After a refreshing siesta, he would go to see his brother Assoweh, his wife Ambaro, and their latest child, Diraneh."

Farther off, a few meters away from the assembly, the village urchins were playing cops and robbers. Using sheep jaws as pistols, the former were yelling at the latter as they ran after them:

"Stop! Stop! Hands up!"

At the same moment, Rayaleh Abaneh had the Wise Men on the edge of their seats:

"Imagine for a moment what happened next . . . No, don't say a word, you are not going to believe me . . . well . . . here is what happened: when Jilaal woke up, he no longer knew a word of our own language, don't you find that strange?" Murmurs were heard here and there. The audience was visibly troubled. Many, unable to follow the *okal*'s story line, pondered a chaplet of questions.

"Do you mean that he had lost the use of his tongue?" ventured a graying Wise Man who had been an infantryman in the last colonial war.

"Honorable Sage, I never said that; it is that Jilaal no longer speaks the same language we all do, as for speaking, he speaks . . . quite strangely!"

Never in the memory of the Issa patriarchs had a mystery been so complete. Who had ever heard of a Bedouin of marriageable age being suddenly stricken by an illness so inconceivable that he would forget his mother tongue? The only one he had ever known. And what demonic language was he speaking in its stead? He who had never gone to any school, not even Koranic school!

"By Allah the Omnipotent, what then is this language that has bewitched him?" cried a Wise Man encased in a caftan the color of the dregs of red wine. And Rayaleh Abaneh admitted his helplessness:

"In Dasbiou, nobody understands his gibberish, including Dirir, the schoolteacher."

Another Wise Man, who until then had been muttering paternosters with a chaplet in his right hand, broke into the now animated discussion:

"*Sallawaad,* it is a sign from the Spirits! By Abdelkadir Jilani, this cannot be taken lightly! This man is possessed, upon my word as a believer who prays five times a day!" Muted turmoil in the assembly. Murmurs rise to the heavens. Rayaleh Abaneh seemed to have lost a little of his loquaciousness. By contrast, the village urchins continued their child's play.

Following the meeting of the Wise Men, the deputy police chief of Dasbiou sought the help of a few friends in order to shed some light on the affair tormenting the villagers. A police inspector dispatched to the scene from the crime investigations unit revealed only part of the key to the mystery. This civil servant, a former student in ethnology at the Catholic University of Ghent in Belgium, succeeded in placing Jilaal's new language. For the inspector, there was no possible doubt: this man was speaking Creole. How was it possible? And why not, in that case, Afar, Amharic, or Arabic? Besides, it was unbelievable: Jilaal had never set foot in a big city, Creole or not.

The deputy chief, ever active any time he could profit from a public matter, summoned from the capital any volunteers who could speak Creole. A Martinican schoolteacher and Freemason from Fort-de-France. A Guyanese physical therapist. A cook from Réunion who was probably Tamil. A Haitian diplomat, smitten with the poetry of Aimé Césaire and married to a local girl. A very handsome Guadeloupean soldier from Gosier. Finally, a few young people who admitted shyly and not without shame their scant knowledge in the field.

The diagnosis was as dry as the weather report: Jilaal spoke Creole perfectly. A rich and colorful Creole, neither too technical nor too abstract. They detected, however, a few archaic, even anachronistic expressions.

"*Isi menm sé komin Vauclin,*" were Jilaal's first words.

Quite moved, the Martinican translated with joy:

"It's unthinkable. He claims to be from Vauclin, a small town in Martinique!" he added meticulously.

The crowd was transfixed. With bloodshot eyes, Rayaleh Abaneh suddenly began to threaten:

"Ji-laal O-kieh, will you start talking like everyone else!"

Silence from the one questioned, who was neither a prophet nor a poet.

The Martinican, in order to be completely sure, asked one last question:

"*Sa ou fè?*"

"*Mwen la ka tyenbe.*"

"He says he is well," continued the translator, full of enthusiasm.

"*Mwen kon chouval la ka galopé, mwen vini la Matinik,*" sang Jilaal to himself.

"I gallop like a horse, I come from Martinique."

No longer listening to the Martinican Wenceslas' precious translations, Rayaleh, mad with rage, spat on the ground and concluded acrimoniously, "This man is insane!"

"Insane! Insane!" repeated the Wise Men in chorus, not all of whom were being candid.

"Insane! Insane!" echoed the crowd.

The subject in question, fathoming not one single word of their perorations, continued to hum:

"Chouval la ka galopé
Chouval la ka kuri
Chouval la ka volé
Mwen chapé adan soleye
Mwen volé adan lannuit . . ."

(A horse that gallops
A horse that runs
A horse that flies
I escaped in the sun
I flew in the night . . .)

The council of Wise Men no longer had any reason to exist. The patriarchs returned to their affairs. The assistant commissioner invited the Creole colony to his home. At table, only Wenceslas seemed lost in his linguistic reveries. After a brief exchange of civilities, they left as discreetly as they had come a good five hours earlier.

In Dasbiou, life returned to normal. Except that at Place de la Gare, in front of Goffané café, Jilaal Okieh hums his eternal monologue:

"Lagye mwen, lagye mwen,
Vauclin sé peyi
Matinik sé peyi mwen
Mwen cheche soleye . . ."

(Let me go, let me go,
Vauclin is my home,
Martinique is my country,
I seek the sun . . .)

THE CORYPHAEUS OF THE COLONY

What is most probable is that we tend to go where we
do not wish to go, and that we tend to do what we would
not wish to do, and that we live and die in a completely
different manner than we would ever wish with
no hope of any kind of recompense.

—Arthur Rimbaud

Gastien Moteur is an enterprising man. He calls himself a builder in the great tradition of Ferdinand de Lesseps (his all-time favorite hero after Christ). He is accompanied by a young man with red hair, a pocked face, and shoulders too broad for his little squirrel-sized head: his longtime associate and whipping boy. In Bordeaux, ideas teemed in Gastien's head to the point that he could no longer sleep a wink, which didn't much please his wife. Odette is a tall, stout brunette without any particular penchants except for the memories she carries of her native Morvan.

Since their arrival in our country—somewhere in the tropics, along the line that goes from Guatemala to the island of Guam in the Pacific, passing through so-called French Guinea, Gabon, and Cape Gwardafui—they have tried very hard, without much apparent success, to change our ways. Gastien swore to himself that he would correct our defective mores, that he would cleanse the grease from our heads (his favorite expression). He says that he has a million projects to implement for our sole well-being. Our country is well suited for that because it is as unsullied as the skin of a newborn baby, as spotless as the peel of a ripe fruit. The country is rich in natural resources and empty of competitors (to butt heads with), he says.

Had he not brought along with him in his suitcases a few indispensable books for carrying out his many projects? Much later, I saw with my own eyes a handyman's manual, a missal, a cookbook, a small picture dictionary, and Mme Odette's unavoidable photo albums. That's it. Truth be told, I suspect that Gastien does not really know how to read very well. Oh, I swear, if he were to read more often, my entire life would be changed. For sure, I would work a lot less. And why doesn't he hunt meerkats like his compatriots?

"Zoko," he often says, pointing his index finger at me, "you ain't like all the others, are ya, my little Zoko-Zokomotive . . . you got somethin' in that noggin a yours . . ."

"Yessir," I mumbled.

"Lissen to me, Zoko. Ya got more upstairs than the others, 'cept y'ain't got what's most important, like an education . . ."

"Yessir," I replied automatically.

"As I was sayin' yesterday to the whole European colony over at Father Urbain de Frouville's durin' drinks, human bein's is ninety percent guts and ten percent heart. The guy that takes chances is a real man. It's guts that counts. All the rest is fairy tales."

"Yessir."

"'Course, everyone agreed with me, even Father Urbain, and that tells ya somethin'. The women clapped for me, and Odette first. Ain't that flatterin'? Do women clap in your country?"

"'Course, sir."

"I added that if this country is what it is today, it's 'cause of men like me. Ninety percent guts and ten percent heart, it's flair that ya gotta have!"

"Yessir."

"Go on, my little Zoko, go get me my bottle and call M. Raoul Prudhomme, get him outta bed. He must be gettin' vulgar readin' that smut."

So I went off to look for M. Gastien's associate. On the way there, I spied Mme Odette on the veranda displaying the photo album to the servant with mother-of-pearl eyes, the ravishing Dahabo. Ever since her arrival, Mme Odette, to the great displeasure of M. Gastien, has incessantly described the Morvan countryside, its copses caressed by mist, its rotting earth, its somber woods, its meandering roads, its little chapels. But how to convey a precise idea of the countryside with yellowed photos, aged by time and lack of care? As for me, every time she questions me about her country, I appeal to my own common sense—I bury myself in my usual silence and let Mme Odette dream. On the other hand, that sweet and ravishing Dahabo showers her with futile questions: "What is a valley, Madame?" "Exactly what is the Morvan?" "Is it always freezing in your country?" And Odette, trembling all over, her throat tight with emotion, provides endless details. She will rise, visibly reinvigorated by the keen interest that her tales arouse in her young and beautiful servant (just between us, Dahabo reminds me of a Matisse odalisque), and return with the atlas under her arm so as to explain latitudes and longitudes to her, equinoxes, atolls, Venus, the Moon, and the phenomenon of tides. They will remain for hours on end conversing together, clumsily drawing valleys and rivers. They will laugh a lot as well.

M. Raoul was reading *Secrets of the Red Sea* in bed when I approached him. He raised his big, bulging fish eyes and looked me over.

"So, secretive Zoko! What the hell have you got to tell me that's so damned important?"

Clearly, here is someone who knows nothing about patience. The Elders of my village would have cursed him forever. At home, when a man says to his wife, "Cursed, three times cursed," they are permanently separated. Deep inside, I could hardly bear the fact that this man, himself a subaltern, would speak to me in such a condescending tone. I now attach great importance to the subtleties of language. I rage inwardly every time someone is disrespectful to me.

M. Raoul crossed the threshold of the sitting room, and I followed him like his shadow. M. Gastien got up, welcomed him with a friendly poke, and invited him to have a drink. This is when M. Gastien gets witty either by making fun of us ("poor uneducated blacks") or by teasing his worthy and gloomy associate. Nevertheless, with his booming voice, he never forgets, so to speak, to pay fraternal homage to the race of builders without whom—once again—the country would not be this haven of peace, extolled over the seven seas as the land of milk and honey. Yes sir, thanks to our efforts, this land is a salubrious haven, a peaceful and suave oasis! Amen.

One evening when he was tipsy after his sixth glass of rum, he came over to confide in me. He had become boorish, just as he did each time he had hit the bottle too much.

"You know, my little Zoko, I can tell you everything. You let me do that, won't you? I'm sure I can tell you everything, my little Zoko. It's not for nothin' that you're the wiliest native I know, eh? (Silence; he's breathing hard. Booming voice again.) Well, I'm puttin' aside a little nest egg. You know what this money'll be for—guess, you little donkey! To raise a statue to my name for my village in the Gironde. A statue of marble with the inscription, 'On behalf of our grateful fatherland, our community is proud to place on this pedestal its son, Gastien Moteur, explorer and builder, who died in the land of the Barbarians.'"

I was stunned. Petrified. So M. Gastien was harboring dreams of grandeur with the shape and colors of the Empire. Maybe he had dreamed of a display dedicated only to himself at the Colonial Exposition, which had just ended in Paris? I knew he was a bit crazy, but I admit he greatly surprised me with his idea of a Napoleonic statue.

From my kitchen I can hear their bursts of laughter. Gastien presides over the company. To hear this kind of vaginal-sounding laughter, I wouldn't be surprised if Mme Odette, who had joined them, were already fairly tipsy. As for M. Gastien . . .

THE SEASCAPE PAINTER AND
THE WIND DRINKER

I indolently inhabit the ruin that I am.

—Louis Calaferte

One paints the sea as a vocation, the other drinks the wind out of dereliction; both of them are unemployed. Badar and Dabar have as their friend a sculptor of dreams who is just as ragged as they are. The more they see each other, the less they see of the rest of society. Others are mobilized to defend the country. The uncivil war rages around them. But Badar and Dabar don't see it that way. There's a reason: they tower head and shoulders over the others. One of them is a seascape painter, the other a drinker of wind. They stutter in the closed chamber of their preoccupations. They are busy with the object of their creation from the first glimmer of morning to the onset of twilight. The sculptor follows their artistic path with a vigilant and even sensual eye. He gives lessons in dignity to the two companions: clean shirt, impeccable bearing, pleasant smile, total communion with the entourage . . . Who would bet on the creations of Badar and Dabar?

They evoke the shared pain that takes root in despair. The country is in a whirl. And then there's the person who calls from Canada every time he is drunk, every time he has drunk too much. And that half-conscious intellectual who fulminates against the congealed atavisms of his society, who mumbles about an aborted life, a half dream, a whisper of life, a life tanned under the patriarchal sun. And the bald moon that smiles viciously, the moon with saffron-colored eyes.

The drinker of wind has composed a sketch, or a playlet as he calls it, entitled *A Study of Khat in D-Muncher.* And nobody got it, not even the poor little play on words. Poor wind drinker, he who has ambitions of writing a requiem for the country's fifteenth anniversary! Goddammit, why compose anything, since no one will hear it anyway? Why ruin one's health? Nonetheless, he only has to cry his fill of tears if he is sad. And yet, so many people are sad here (and elsewhere). There's nothing left to do except to grope his way out of the maze. He only has to shuffle back to his bed to sleep as he awaits his beautiful death.

The sculptor works right in the middle of the neighborhood. He carves recalcitrant trunks with billhooks. Later, he will give form to a series of venerable busts. He would like to assemble all the individuals who have counted in this country. He had decided to dream usefully. He would fight with the moon if necessary in order to represent the slightly sour humidity of eternal summer. A rump here, a bust and a camber there, the curve of a calf over there, and the erect nipple of a breast beneath fabric . . . All of the fellows in the country are seeing the light without finery or frills. Who was it who said that one could die of despair? In any case, the sculptor makes himself useful in these times of uncivil war. The sculptor labors as he waits for peace. And the sweet milk of peace.

One is a seascape painter, the other a wind drinker; their only friend is the sculptor of dreams who knows how to make himself useful. They are suspended part-timers who wanted to grab life by the horns. But the country has the defeated face of hard times. The uncivil war looks like an apocalypse under the patricidal sun.

During history's grave moments, speech falters, confidence crumbles; one attends to the most urgent things first, that is, to survive in whatever setting (even if it's a quagmire where the moon no longer shines, or where the imperial sun no longer has any say). Don't count on Badar, Dabar, and Nadar the sculptor to recant; they stopped singing palinodes long ago. They are formed of sincere clay. Simple as granite.

"Nature has endowed us with a fiery temperament, we are easily offended," says Badar, eyeing Nadar scornfully.

"What do you expect? It's the privilege of the weak."

DETOUR

"The rabble of the powerful is encased in its own pride, isn't it?" remarks Nadar, both perfidious and mocking.

"He who farts need not breathe, as my defunct grandfather would say."

"Stop philosophizing, Badar."

"I'm not philosophizing at all. I'm talking in the style of some of those African authors who imitate Chinua Achebe."

"We don't give a damn about them. Just talk like Nadar and me and not like some old book published with the support of the ACCT or Edicef."

"He who rises need not rest his ass on a chair."

"When you come back to earth, we will be able to get some work done," threatens Dabar.

"Let me remind you that you have a painting to finish," says Nadar.

Certainly, there is no need to speak in exactly the same way, but, for all that, do you need to multiply languages to infinity? The country has already endowed itself with four languages: two official ones because they are foreign (French for distinction and Arabic for cash from the Persian Gulf) and two national ones because they are indigenous.

In a dusty back courtyard, rubbish, rocks, and iron scraps melt into an amalgamation to form blocks of anthracite that are part totem, part tool. Nadar sculpts and Badar paints while Dabar looks on and asks questions.

"So what are you doing?"

"I'm painting."

"So what are you painting?"

"Plateaus constrained by enormous cliffs within the collapsed plains of more plateaus and basalt mountain chains."

"But what else?"

"Seventy percent humidity."

"How's that?"

"My dear Dabar, my paintings are alive, they breathe, inhale, and exhale carbon dioxide just like Nadar's sculptures, or like you and me."

"But what else?"

"From October to April, it's the cool season (25 degrees Celsius); from May to September, it's the torrid season, insufferable even for the indigenous people: 45 degrees Celsius."

"My word, it's a weather report!"

"Even better, it's my painting: a medium radiating with life."

"But what else?"

"Well, let's say sparse and irregular rain."

"You surprise me every day."

"There! The painting is finished. Act like an art dealer, look at it with an expert eye, neglect nothing, neither the iconographic message, nor the aesthetic emotion, nor even the a posteriori ideological dimension of the unfinished work. Go ahead, I'm waiting for an assessment; tell me, what do you think?"

"Give me a second at least."

"Quick, an opinion."

"For sure, you will always surprise me. I can't see your damned painting and besides I don't know anything about art. You're talking to me like a tourist brochure and you're asking me to judge something that's invisible."

The painter with baguette legs has stopped taking his friend for an art critic. They resume their former discussions about overpaid hatchet men, about gun-wielding arms raised, about humanity violated. Very clever, the one who can read tomorrow in today's open palm. The sky meets the sea: it's dark. Night is going to fall.

"In any case, one thing is certain; we are the failure of metaphor and the frustration of the author." Nadar is the first to open fire.

"Does that mean then that we are condemned to self-mutilation and silence?"

"Well, nothing is more comforting to people than to have no opinion whatsoever. It really is the bitter truth."

"Rimbaud quested after an 'I' that was at once Self and Other. As for us, we seek an 'I' in the undifferentiated 'We,' right, Badar?"

"Our leisurely discussions here are a joke as long as gun-wielding arms are being raised everywhere. The local Pol Pots have had their machetes sharpened for a long time."

"Heads turbaned or helmeted, Hissène Habré look-alikes, imitators of Massoud the Afghani, copies of Jonas Savimbi or of John Garang, our local Mad Maxes ask nothing better than to demolish the power of clan leaders and other avuncular types."

"A thousand seasons in hell! We have seen a parade of a thousand infernal seasons. Rimbaud can't top that."

"He would roll over in his grave if he saw what's happening on our county's doorstep."

"Forget about your Rimbaud. We have nothing to do with that fellow from the Ardennes."

"And you, stop your bloated frog's laugh!"

"Well, do you think we could at least invoke Dante?" asks Nadar, losing none of his morbid humor.

"Of course. We already live in the third world of the third world."

"Yes. Let's just send him off to the border with Somalia," Dabar adds through tight lips.

A FERROUS TALE

The sea is a savanna of water.
—Tchicaya U Tam'si

Over its entire length, it will stretch 784 kilometers. It will cut across deserts, plains, savannas, and high plateaus. A condensation of History. It will stretch out. Two parallel lines of blood will join two countries and a thousand landscapes. A difficult pregnancy: it will take twenty years before it becomes useful. It will be born one day in 1897—first on graph paper. It will trample the downtrodden of modernity. It will leave the land of thirst. It will climb, climb, climb, to an altitude of 2,350 meters. It will climb from the slack bluish sea to the foothills invaded by dark green eucalyptus:

> It will cross the real country.
> It will cross the dream country.

From the outset, it constructed history: it stacked up dates and military exploits; it compiled successes and failures. It built a castle of memory where every clan, every protagonist—French engineers, Swiss planners, Afar sultans, Somali workers, Abyssinian soldiers . . . —could come to shop at the memories on display. Statistics were on its side, irrefutable figures, solid as the steel that supports it: 784 kilometers long and reaching an altitude of 2,350 meters, 1,355 bridges, 31 works of art, a stockpile of balance sheets, several hundred million in capital. How many human lives lost? No one kept count.

It will bear the label "Conceived and Built by Great French Genius." People will come to auscultate it, photograph it, ask its opinions on the psychology of the autochthonous peoples,

DETOUR

on the latest effects of the trampoline of history: on Adoua,* "pacification," on the 1001 conquests of the Abyssinian ogre, etc.

They will find its older brothers, American uncles coming straight from the frontier of the Far West:

It will cross the real country.
It will cross the dream country.

It came charging out one day in 1897. It terrorized a certain number of usually impassive nomads. The two rails traced one of Dante's rings. It wounded the real country. Just one example: at the place called Jab Issa,** the warriors of that tribe massacred the railroad workers who insisted on laying the perfidious tracks of the monster over the shrine of a venerated ancestor. The vengeance of the colonial troops was consonant with their reputation. It would be three years before work could begin again.

It will span wadis. It will dig tunnels into the flanks of bister-colored mountains. It will count the crackling of stones exploding under the halo of a fulminating sun. Tumefaction. It will consume the heart of the region born on the fourth day of creation. Putrefaction. The Issas, overwhelmed, will find themselves with their backsides in the dust. Then they will raise their heads—*Ciisow Sarakaa! Ciisow Sarakaa!*† They will once again rouse their scattered brethren, they will launch raids. They will launch razzias. The monster will be vanquished for a while. A sign will warn: "Work Stopped." The autochthonous people will show themselves to be tough. The sun will defecate on the steel viscera of the comatose monster.

Haltingly, the work will begin again. The fires of the bivouac will be relit. A little virgin moon will make apologies in place of the solar star. The autochthonous people will become

*The historic defeat of the Italians by the Abyssinian emperor Menelik II.
**The Defeat of the Issa.
†"Rise, Issas, Rise!"

disheartened. Their caravans will pale in comparison to the noisy, rattling competition from the metallic monster. Prayers will go up to God in all the languages of the country. While the project's two Swiss planners, Ilg and Chefneux, will gloat. It will follow its projected route. Paris will keep a greedy eye on its progress. There will be surprise at the duration of the lull. Pacification will have taught a lesson to the hotheads. Sacks of dates will be given to the cooperative nomads:

It will cross the real country.
It will cross the dream country.

It has marked space. It has excised the earth. It has marked men. It has marked their languages. Little towns have sprung up along its route as though in ceremonious greeting.

The interpreter for the Whites said:

"Venerable assembly, White people wish you no harm. All they ask is a corridor through your territory: just enough to lay two steel rails."

The assembly said nothing. The interpreter spread his legs and said:

"The White people ask for this little space contained between my legs."

The assembly shattered into confusion. Half recognized the insignificance of the request. The other half remained wary, ready to brandish arms.

The value of sworn oaths diminished with the speed of the engine. Seeds of doubt found receptive hearts in the surrounding land. The rapacious pragmatism of the railway company triumphed. The extent of confusion among the autochthonous elders was confirmed through the ages:

It has crossed the sunburned land.
It has crossed the haggard land.

It will keep advancing. It will leave behind the tiny French colony on the edge of the Red Sea. Earthquakes set off by dynamite to blast the tunnels: the earth will resist in the land of the Rift Valley. The dromedaries will mock the articulated monster. It will keep advancing. It will experience immobility in the little plain of Galilee. It will leave Aïchaa. It will feel the flamboyance of the void at the entrance to the great Hadagalla plain. It will come out on the side where the termite hills are.

The last handful of adversaries has not yet had its final say. Skulking men, knives between their teeth, have attacked the bivouacs. White engineers have perished under white steel. Menelik, Emperor of Ethiopia, was displeased. His punitive expeditions gave no quarter. Corrupt apocalyptic atmosphere. Thus . . .

It has crossed the sunburned land.
It has crossed the haggard land.

It will leave the desert. It will leave the savanna. The landscape will trade its brown ochers for a gamut of greens. It will build the biggest city in the region: Dire-Dawa cramped between two mountains. The sky will darken. Great clouds will loom over it. It will rain as usual: a tropical rain, violent and short. It will stop to catch its breath and gather strength. The workers will procure fresh supplies.

It trembled at the sight of the first river: the Awash. It labored near Awash (the city), the land is basalt—the population is Afar, Issa, or Orgabo. It was battered. It was sabotaged. The sun snickered by day, the hyenas threatened at nightfall. It was pillaged. They almost rang the death knell . . .

It has crossed the inflamed land.
It has crossed the fissured land.

Drumrolls: it will reach Nazareth, the well named. It will furrow the meandering flanks of the Choa mountains. Menelik will rejoice. Paris will heave a sigh. Addis Ababa, the new flower of the ever-conquering Abyssinian Empire will smile at it.

A FERROUS TALE

Addis Ababa, the gleaming capital, will pour libations with the sweat of its workers. A little white moon will open the festivities. A momentous day: champagne, palm wine, Abyssinian mead, soda for the austere Muslims. Canon salvos from the garrison of Entoto . . . The line will be opened June 2, 1917. Long live the Franco-Ethiopian Railway Company!

It has transformed the notion of time and space, the direction of history. It has imposed upon the autochthonous people. They called it *firhoun* and *Ibliss*.* And unable to ignore it, they have adopted it . . . in their own words:

The steel that advances (the train)
The iron that supports it (the rails)
And the one that answers them (the posts)
Just what are these metals that invade the land?
It spits, it groans, it stinks.
But with it, you cover the distance.
Here in the morning, in the evening quite far away
At milking time in the encampment of your clan
To share with them the milk
still foaming.**

*Names of the devil.
**This Bedouin song, as well as framework of this story, were borrowed from an article by the Djiboutian journalist Ali Moussa Iyé, "The Dbjibouto-Ethiopian Railway, or the Saga of the Far East," *Autrement*, no. 21 (January 1987).

II

RETURN

PAGES TORN FROM

THE LAND WITHOUT SHADOWS

.

A WOMAN AND A HALF

Our women are beautiful, we should display them.
Does one veil roses?

—Kateb Yacine

Marwo, a young woman worn down by life, flees the shanty-town, a large chunk of humanity living in sludge and rustic ennui. Marwo flees her degrading father who wants to give her away to a toothless old man. She flees hatred of the old goat, she flees harassment from Chireh, her elder brother, henchman of the political police, conquistador of naked violence, reveler in the marcescent bodies of victims and great aesthete of torture.

Marwo flees the complicity of the serenely senile father certain of his rights, and of the simian-like satyr, her satrap brother. She flees the indifference of the shantytown, the mothers who invite her to bow to the will of the patriarch. She flees a fate as bitter as wormwood.

She rose at the outposts of day, well before the muezzin had blown into his mezzo sax, and while daylight was still germinating in the fields of night. This dawn is pregnant with hope.

Where to go? She fidgets with impatience.

"I'll turn to the old *askari*,"* she tells herself as she prepares for a nocturnal meeting.

I'm leaving the divided and divisive shantytown, I'm leaving the trash heap of fractured lives, the inconsistent silhouettes, the pack of killers coughing over raw-boned whores, the tribe of the sleepy strewn in the trash-lined alleys.

*Soldier of the East African colonial armies.

I'm leaving the night mist that staggers as it flees the un-furling sun. I'm leaving night punched through by day, the ten-ebrous rhizomes.

Turn to whom? Seek shelter with Haybé, the old *askari,* the old uncle retired in the bush, the word seeker with a constant appetite for meaning. I will go to look for a new life, an aborted life, I will go part the waters of my freedom.

Haybé will take me under his wing, dote on me and rock me like a baby. Haybé, the motionless eagle, the rock and the mineral of meaning, beautiful constancy of faith rediscovered, Haybé of enchanted heart, of animated word.

Marwo, tall in stature, firm and angular of haunch, of swelling breast, is, moreover, an excellent walker, a marathoner from before Olympia. She crossed the desert, then the desic-cated oasis, then the savanna with its teeming termite mounds. She traveled a way with smugglers, cameleers who have been making this trip for centuries, Sinbads of the sands with soles of wind. Travelers who tire even the earth, the mirages, and the stars themselves. Seekers of horizons. Profiles erect as an "I," camels ungainly and proud, foam on their chops. And the jumble of goods: rolls of cloth, bars of salt, sticks of incense, packets of provisions, of tobacco, boxes of munitions . . .

They stopped to eat under a tree, an acacia, tree of the poor. They swallowed some steamed rice and a handful of dates. A chatterbox was chain-smoking and pestering Marwo with a stream of questions:

"Flower of the faubourg, where are you going like this?"

Silence on the part of the addressee.

"Ebony eyes, the bush is not for people like you. You will leave behind bits of flesh, shreds of cloth, on my word as a cameleer! It will harden your baby heart. Before the first down-pours of Jilal,* you will return to the city among the gaudy, on my word as a cameleer!"

---

*The rainy season.

A WOMAN AND A HALF

"I did well to leave the buzzing flies behind."

She wanted to add that she had also done well to leave behind the detestable figure of the father, but she abstains, knowing full well that the cameleer could denounce her without the least remorse. For a pack of cigarettes, he would no doubt return her to her father's lair, bound hand and foot. He would not hesitate for one second, convinced as he was of his rights as a male with a well-filled scrotum between his legs. For a camel, he would kill her without batting an eyelid.

Because the camel is everything. Anything beyond the herd is the elsewhere, faraway and unknown, the limbo of the void. The camel is the gold standard, the animal with a thousand names, the center of life and the seat of taboos. The female camel is the currency of exchange, and the blood money for a woman is fifty head, or half as much as for a male!

Is Marwo going to adopt an itinerant life in contrast to a dull existence in the gravel of the shantytown? Haybé smiles sensibly, offering Marwo the spectacle of his half-loose teeth. Haybé had invented an original hypothesis that would explain the inequality of the sexes in the society of yesterday and today. If one were to believe Haybé, one would have to go back to the myth of origins and to what he calls "the first negotiation."

"What is that about, Uncle?" asks Marwo, as agitated as a cover on a boiling pot.

"This is the myth to which I have added my own personal fancy; besides, my hypothesis is grounded in common sense . . . Here it is: when WAAQ, the pre-Islamic God of the Somalis, our great creator, gave our Ancestor the camel, the animal of life in the desert, WAAQ asked the Ancestor to sacrifice to him that which was most dear. And the ancestor solemnly replied,

"'I will sacrifice to you an elder son every seven moons.'

"And WAAQ acquiesced and then disappeared.

"Upon returning to his encampment, the Ancestor joined the assembly of the elders under the tutelary tree and informed the conclave of the pact with WAAQ. But the meeting was tumultuous and lasted for eight days and as many nights. Not everyone agreed on the terms and of course there were no women among the elders.

RETURN

"Guess what they decided to do, my little Marwo?"

"I don't know, Uncle, it is you who knows how to tell all to the last detail, don't you?"

"In their madness, the men had taken the risk of lying to WAAQ, and instead of offering the sacrifice of the eldest son of the Ancestor, they instead offered the youngest daughter, a child resembling a figurine with a head no bigger than a thumb."

"Before today, I had never heard such a thing."

"That does not surprise me at all. For a long time, men had been sealing female orifices, sewing mouths and genitals shut. And yet, without their mothers, daughters, or wives, men are the dwarf palms of the shriveled oasis; men are the scum of the dust, while women are the humus of the earth."

Marwo knows her uncle, his quest for the word, his taste for parables, the preeminence of a sometimes strangely pagan moral exigency. Does Haybé not live with imagination, that beggar woman of anonymous streets?

She had fled the fractured beings of the shantytown, all of them ruled by her father's authority and especially by her brother's army rabble. She had chosen the road opposite that of all the Bedouins for whom the attraction of the city was as to a precious gem. She had left the tedium of the shanty-town behind. She had found refuge with the uncle, purveyor of meaning, the teacher who clears the way—as he puts it—for the silken future of children to come.

It was still a time when every young man had to prove himself by ravishing the young woman who pleased him from the encampment of her tribe and even out from under her father's roof if necessary. The suitor thus had to risk his life simply in order to show everyone the flames corroding his heart. Doubtless, the game was worth the effort?

Bogoreh was on the trail of the too beautiful and too graceful Raïsso. Like a general on campaign, he had been studying his plan for weeks and weeks. The location of the huts and the animal enclosures in his sweetheart's encampment were familiar to him. The number of young warriors in charge of protecting the clan as well as their martial habits counted among his primary preoccupations. He knew that they were all marvelous in battle.

Bogoreh was also a fearsome warrior, a monster of energy and ruse and sometimes of cruelty, who had also killed many times in combat. And yet, Bogoreh was proud as a peacock. He rejected his father's call for caution and the advice of his friends who suggested that he await the most propitious moment for his enterprise: when the men would all be exhausted by the year's hardest work.

After the rains, this work involved reconstructing the wells, leaving to scout out new pastures, discovering wadis revived by the rains, and finally choosing the areas that would hold up under the scorching sun for the longest time. First the pastures would be flavescent, then gray, before cracking under hoof and withering like peeling skin.

Just before this vital work, the herders would leave to sell a portion of their livestock in the neighboring villages so as to buy the most common goods (salt, sugar, tobacco, black tea, grain . . .) but also cloth (often cotton fabric) and, more rarely, novelty items (soap or jewelry).

RETURN

Bogoreh was a man in a hurry. He did not want to wait for the end of the rains. He did not want to wait for the period of the year's hardest work, for animals to be sold, for animals to be milked, for meat to cure, for cream to be churned into clarified butter . . . in sum, he did not want to wait for all the work that preludes the rainy season.

He no longer wanted to wait. Even more so because the herders returning from the animal markets at Hadagallah or Aïcha-la-Bigote were bringing gifts to the young virgins.

It was a time for rejoicing. Girls and boys teased each other until late on nights when the moon was full. Dances. Songs. All-night vigils around a fire. Wrestling matches. Tales and riddles. Hide-and-seek. The word regained its pedigree. Everywhere people were telling stories. Narrating. Ranting. Raving. Improvising. Martial mores faded for a moment . . . Attention had to be paid to lyricism because young women were always sensitive to poetry. Bogoreh was restless with impatience.

Just yesterday he had met the radiant Raïsso on the bank of a river. Habad, Khaireh, Miganeh, and Dembil, Raïsso's four brothers, were standing guard, protecting their sister: amber-skinned, slender of figure as though sculpted by the most gifted artisan, long of neck with shy doe eyes. Raïsso had not even deigned to direct a smile toward him. Who does this young goat take himself for? He has just become a cameleer and he already thinks he's a real man? Hoping that Habad, the harebrained eldest, champion of the dagger, jealous and gloomy, would not pick a fight with him. The situation would quickly deteriorate. Hoping that Khaireh, the malicious younger brother, the rancorous outlaw, would not push his three brothers to uselessly provoke this boastful Bogoreh. Hoping that the volcanic Miganeh, Habad's epigone, would not take a sudden dislike to him. He's really capable of ruining everything, that one. Ah! Dembil, the youngest, the most sensible, Dembil, my favorite. Luckily, he's not one to pick a fight at just any time!

By the grace of the prodigious Creator, there was no fight. The four brothers had a lot to do: water the family's large herd. Perhaps none of them had noticed the ploys of Bogoreh

Foureh, son of Foureh Obsieh Guireh—warrior and man of
words known in the land of the black rocks—and of Khorane
Robleh. As soon as the four brothers and the sister had left the
river, the intrepid Bogoreh began to follow them while maintaining some distance so as not to attract attention.

In the encampment, besides Raïsso's four brothers, there
were their father Idleh Miad, his three wives, his eighteen
children, his seven brothers and their respective families.
Grandchildren were more numerous than beads on a string.
Some of the grandfathers were as robust as pubescent boys: one
of them, an octogenarian, was recovering from the effects of a
rattlesnake bite. In the encampment there was also a boy come
from who knows where, of an ethnicity quite different from
our own, but who spoke our language like any of us, old men
included.

Back then, it was Dembil who had taught him the rudi-
ments of our language. Since then, Aptidon* (we had given him
the appropriate name under the circumstances) had adopted
his new identity perfectly. Dembil and Aptidon agreed on everything: they played together, watched over the sheep from the
age of five, then the dromedaries at age fifteen, sang on nights
when the moon was full, teased the girls . . .

If Bogoreh had any serious competitors, it was in the person
of Aptidon, who had the merit of having conquered a consider-
able part of the tribe by his arduous work, his availability, his
lyricism on feast days, and his courage in combat. In addition,
Dembil would be his most fervent supporter. As for the other
three brothers, their opinion was not really known. Especially
the eldest, who had the right to pronounce himself ahead of all
the other members of the extended family (right after the father). If by chance Habad did not state his opinion, then watch
out! A thousand years of Gehenna. Infertility for him and for
his future wife. No repose here on earth. No repose in the other
world. Not to mention his herd, which would only continue to

---

*Literally, "he who wants a maternal uncle," meaning his mother has
no brother.

decline in number . . . Who was it who had said that the world would collapse?

The women whispered among themselves that Aptidon was secretly striving to gather the necessary sum in order to win the angelic Raïsso of almond eyes and hourglass shape. What a handsome couple they would make! They had not counted on Bogoreh, who followed feverishly in Raïsso's wake, suddenly appearing and disappearing like the sun between the clouds.

Bogoreh would soon act, although for the moment he showered his future prey with many a consideration: toothy smiles and sweet—sepia colored—looks each time he chanced to meet her crossing the savanna. Like every sylph, Raïsso hardly set her splendid sole tail–shaped eyes on him. She knew she was being courted, what am I saying? almost venerated by the warrior with teeth filed into triangles. Which gave her a haughty air just as it did to all the other girls of the land.

When Bogoreh followed her, he concentrated on Raïsso's ankles. Happy would be the man who would taste the sumptuous flesh of the little feral female with breasts more firm than a ripe pear, who would inhale her inebriating odors, her sweat, who would plant his seed in the jumble of her idyllic garden and would drink his fill of her opal nectar from its source between her legs . . . Amen!

It was a time when every young man worth his salt had to ravish his future partner, when the earth was clad in its green cloak, when the railway had not yet made its appearance. God had not yet become this Cerberus that threatens men. Bogoreh had just turned twenty.

Brazier in the sky. Scarlet twilight. The ordinarily white or diaphanous flowers were covered with petals of blood. At the hour when the orycteropus emerges, when filtered shadow—ashen and bister—veils the landscape, Bogoreh decided to slip inside Raïsso's encampment. Nightfall was greeted with the great rending cry of a wounded animal which immediately faded into the surrounding immensity. The entire herd awoke from its crepuscular torpor. Ovines, bovines, kids, and camelids pricked up their ears. As for the dogs, they had already understood the danger.

BRAZIER IN THE SKY

The four brothers took from the encampment a man who was losing a torrent of blood. They placed him under an acacia long enough to resheathe their daggers, wash their hands, and saddle their horses. From their mouths they emitted no sound. A few minutes later, they returned the cadaver to the encampment of Bogoreh's family. Habad, Khaireh, Miganeh, and Dembil saw the Adam's apple of the old oracle Foureh Obsieh rise and fall. Silence de rigueur.

"He only got what he deserved. Who knows what he meant to accomplish. No one should get so infatuated with a woman. May he rest in peace," said Habad, the eldest.

"Leave!" ordered Foureh Obsieh, before adding the proverb that is still in effect today: "A dead man is not worth the sandals on his feet (*Nin dhintey kabixiisa ka roon*)."

THE RUMINANTS OF ROUTINE

In this country of fractured memory, "forgetfulness or unconsciousness are the only guarantees of serenity."
—Rachid Mimouni

(A heavily cadenced, very repetitive music, entrancing like Sufi rhythms, comes to dwell in me, to animate me.)

While I was comparing the Fulani (Peul) in the novel *Burning Grass* by Cyprian Ekwensi to the Somali as they appear in the novels of Nuruddin Farah, and particularly in *From a Crooked Rib*—his very first novel—someone knocked at my door. I hesitate. I linger in my daydreams. Footsteps echo once again in the corridor. Insistent footsteps. Someone was coming for me. Silence . . . Mariam, my nurse, enters without warning:

"Always reading."

I don't really know why, but I heard in the voice of my jailer a panpipe and a drum that took me back to the past. All the same, I answered her through gritted teeth:

"Hum."

"Just another excuse for doing nothing. You really are bone idle. If all patients were like you . . . by the way, what are you up to now?

"I'm thinking about the Fulani," I murmured.

"The what?"

"The Fulani, that's what the Peul are called in some African countries, in Cameroon and Nigeria, for example."

"Your taste for far-off places will be your downfall one of these days," threatened Mariam, who no longer seemed to be listening to my explanations.

It must be said that she stopped listening long ago. She no longer pays any attention to me. For Mariam, I am nothing but an absent being, a bookworm who gnaws on books: bowed neck, glassy, runny eyes, with no expression whatsoever, head buried between the pages. For her, I am the being-in-absence, the bookworm-who-gnaws-on-books, and then there are the others: the ruminants of routine. Evidently, she does not take me seriously. I must confess that it is hard to take me seriously. Do I look thoughtful, with the impassible gaze of the psychoanalyst, the minute gestures of the surgeon, the obvious assurance of the imam at the first prayer of the day in the calm of dawn? And yet, I distress Mariam, an ordinary woman of a country without whimsy completely engrossed in masticating the meager remains of a meal already munched on elsewhere and brought here thanks to the admirable energy of the purveyors of charity. In public, our leaders drip with kindness but share with strict parsimony the offal donated by beneficent societies. She stopped questioning me ages ago; no doubt she has fallen into the long and gray corridors of my imagination; she has landed in front of the changing antechamber of my perception. Resigned, she has settled for helping me with my daily domestic tasks. It was she who insisted on bringing me my three meals, my chamber pot, and my books. Silent, slender, as impalpable as a shadow passing back and forth in front of my window, who enters without warning and without sound, who tries to remind me of the existence of the outside world, the presence of the ruminants of routine, the khat that they chew all day long, and in any case, their fears and their (false) hopes, the cupidity of some, the treachery of others, the singers condemned to remain silent to the end of their days, the young girls who prostitute themselves, relegating to the shadows in an eminently brazen manner the older harlots with buttocks rumpled by misery and the heat . . . She informs me that hornets come to invade the peninsula at nightfall . . . The ruminants of routine are worried: ants cooped up in anthills that are in turn hidden in the incandescent breast of a crater ceaselessly caressed by the limping waves of a sea in flames . . . The ruminants of routine disdain the products of the holy sea. No people has dared to insult the gods of iodized water! To be sure, they will come—of their own accord—to submit, to implore forgiveness, to beg for a few sardines, and to wallow on the beaches reserved until now for passing foreigners, for ex-patriots, for wandering Jews, for the idle unemployed. As for me, I will see them from my window.

Drunk with certainties on the heights of despair, the ruminants let time slide over their bodies. Visibly, time slides over them—but it erodes them deeply. For they are fragile beneath their seamless masks. Life is shaken here more than anywhere else, the earth's crust could not be more fragile and hope is downright threatened.

Mariam, my jailer, cannot fathom any of all that. Good-hearted and simpleminded, after the fashion of the ruminants, she thinks that the sun rises and sets behind the mountains that surround the citadel. Mariam can only fathom the daily and practical tasks: yesterday it was the sheep that had to be let in and out of the fold, the cows to be milked, the men to satisfy; today it is the cooking to be done for the entire clan, the incessant errands, watching after me, and still more males to satisfy and ancestral spirits to celebrate. Still to be endured (besides!) is the ill humor and the proverbial ingratitude of the ruminants of routine, the lascivious looks of the oldest, the caresses of the more daring.

Imprisoned by her gender, more submissive than ever, over and over again—before my very eyes—Mariam has been taken by feverish, hurried ruminants, who have soiled her leather-and-honey-colored thighs with spurts of slimy sperm. These slapdash operators satisfy themselves in a hurry, making way for a buddy just as rushed, maybe on the verge of impotence, who gives up his turn to a beardless youth ignorant of the mysteries of sex. And I, the shut-in, I am divided between sympathy for my warder and my violent urges as a male versed in voyeurism.

THE RUMINANTS OF ROUTINE

As you may have noticed, for the ruminants, everything is done as a group and in haste. A bit in the manner of ants, minus the meticulousness and the taste for work!

I laugh up my sleeve. To think that they treat me with such respect, that they seem attentive to my fate when they put on those sincere pitying airs the few times that they meet me in the street. Some are deeply disconcerted if not frightened to see me, while others discreetly change sidewalks. Absorbed in my reveries, or on the telephone with the great Elsewhere, I do not say a word to them, not even a smile or a nod of greeting. I pay no attention to the pity they feel for my puny person. I do not give an ounce of importance to their aversion either. And yet, an idea has begun to surface in my mind: am I not—in their eyes—irremediably insane? And Mariam, isn't she my prisoner? Could she quite simply be born of my imagination? Am I the only one who still wishes to dream about the land of the ruminants of routine?

But first, who am I?

SOUND MIX

Like prolonged echoes mingling from afar.
—Charles Baudelaire

We are funambulists on the wire of Far Away, our dreams are directed elsewhere. We have the excellent hearing of the lycaon. And magic words resonate like antennas in our ears: Canada-United States-Australia-America-Europe-Holland-Switzerland-Scandinavia-USA. These refrains, all echoes, keep us alive. Ca-na-da-Ca-na-da-Ca-na-da-Ca-na-da . . . Why should we complain, we shades, somber nyctalopic zombies, while our officials, flag bearers and beacons of the Nation, have fled with nothing less than the coffers of the State?

The most educated among us, those who speak an obscure sabir, bring us fresh words each new day, words rich in resonance tumbling over the cascades of Breath, words that snap like a leather whip and that fortify you as only strong alcohol can. These days, our wire has been substantially charged with meanings unknown to us until now. We owe this to a zombie friend—just recently settled over there—who has taken the trouble to send us (by telephone) inebriating echoes to whet our appetites. Oh, we are incapable of drawing an iota of comfort from our real lives. But now we have precious offerings, substantial gifts that we would not be able to find even in the innermost depths of the imaginary of a damned people: Quebec and Ontario, Acadia and Manitoba, among other places. Those are the most memorable delights that one can offer in this season of agony.

Nothing on the horizon, nothing behind us: we are the children of Nothingness. Our muscles are completely anesthetized, our young reason has taken refuge in the farthest corners of our toes, our blood has solidified and evaporated under the sun of this grievous season. We are funambulists on the wire of Far Away. Our world is in advanced deliquescence and releases deleterious gasses.

We also seek, in vain, the location and the formula.

Only the mosque and the Party mike possess the (coveted) right to flood stillborns, deaf-mutes, unemployed fakirs, widows of dissenters, and others agonizing in forced hibernation with litanies such as this:

"Your world is not Here, your world is the great Elsewhere!"

We took it literally. We had to.

With the flair and clairvoyance we know him for, the recently-settled-over-there–zombie telephoned us on the feast of Aïd, just when the entire neighborhood was as sad as a sweltering sunny morning; children are no longer born on that day, the air is so asphyxiating and false. But on precisely that day, our happiness was incommensurable; surely we were happier than on Independence Day, a vulgar, torrid day in June when joy struck down twenty elders with weak hearts and when twenty black rams were run over by green and white vehicles come from who knows where. Insouciance and imprudence. A prelude to misfortunes to come—perhaps. On that day then, our happiness was inordinate when we heard over the grating telephone line this unusual resonance, unknown and inconceivable to us until then. It was vibrant, intoxicating, and very rich. Immediately our hopes rang softly everywhere. In harmony, or almost. Then with a certain violence. And our horizon receded just a bit while we heard the cascade continue.

"And what is the very rich voice saying?

"Wait! Say it again softly: yes we are all hanging on the wire of Hope, yes, we're here, ok, go on . . ."

A deafening thunder beats down on the hovel; the cascade, the decrescendo of the metallic voice ricochets off the walls of zinc and the roofs of aluminum. The echoes of the trumpeter on the telephone increase in our eardrums, fragment, so much that our other senses remain as if demobilized. We became all ears. Although the zombie hung up, our ears remained deaf for a few instants. The length of a shudder.

Nothing but hearing. All of our other senses went on strike. What difference did it make. We learned with the complicity of the telephone and the good will of the newly exiled zombie a brand-new sound, words like new coins, gleaming, along with a piece of Elsewhere that we straightaway appropriated for ourselves. Thus a new hope was born; day was beginning to break. And eggs to hatch. It was nothing yet but a burgeoning; the flowering would doubtless be late. But what difference did it make, we knew that our zombie, with us yesterday, was over there today. On a bottle-green islet, an immaculate sail swollen by the winds carries him above an ultramarine sea with reflections of ivory and gold (he told us) while we were sailing on ashen gray dunes that tire the eyes and legs.

When silence, stillness, and the unparalleled purity of the midnight dew returned, one of the zombies with a marble look asked,

"This new word, this unusual name that he said, what is it?"

We rushed at him as though to crush him, to discharge over him in chorus our daily dose of bitter bile. We paralyzed him with our aggressive—to say the least—cries that spoke volumes about our atavistic impotence. The leader of the zombies, a teacher who has always been in the street, spit right in his face, then without any further ado, sliced the left earlobe of the marble mask so as to mark it for life.

"He is in Sas-kat-che-wan, Sas-kat-che-wan, remember this name forever, otherwise watch out for the other ear, poor fellow!"

The name, it is true, was a particularly juicy substance for us. We adopted it. We turned it over in our mouths until our jaws got tired, until our saliva dried up, until we choked. Finally, we were rich; we now possessed a dripping wet melody in our hunting bags, a melody which brightened the most deserted corners of the leper house and which no one—not even the Party leaders—could confiscate from us. We had acquired another name, we had claimed a virgin territory, a new world. Well, what a name! What wealth! What an appropriation!

Truly an entire universe. We sung it again in chorus in order to learn it by heart, to occupy it definitively:

"Sas-kat-che-wan-Sas-kat-che-wan-Sas-kat-che-wan-Sas-kat-che-wan-Sas-kat-che-wan-Sas-kat-che . . ."

And one last time from the beginning:

"Ca-na-da-Aus-tra-lia-On-ta-rio-USA-Que-bec-Sas-kat-che-wan-Ca-na-da-Aus-tra . . ."

FILTHY ASKAR

On the road, not far from the Crossroads of the Martyrs, a dust-covered army truck is parked across the road, blocking access to vehicles of all makes and functions. A crowd gathers around this makeshift barricade. Men, women, and a pleiad of children, issued from the nearby Mahmoud Harbi School, come running. It is almost noon. The sun shoots rays sharper than glass shards. The colorful crowd, loud, overheated by the scorching temperature, presses even closer together around the barricade, completely blocking the passage of any car. Part of the excited crowd spills over onto the sidewalks. Spontaneous scuffles pit backside against backside, or head against head as in a rugby match. Some girls complain: since they are too small, they can't see the spectacle.

A bit farther on, at the corner of Gabobé-Sanngué Street, drivers bite their lips with impatience and compete in honking to take revenge on the crowd for its sudden irruption into the street. The noise crescendos. There, women in gray ruin their vocal chords bawling louder than their neighbors. Next to them, a dog-faced policeman is hoarse from barking at a recalcitrant driver who unsuccessfully tries to break through the human barricade. Already, an ambulance can be heard approaching with its two-toned ballet.

But what kind of show is attracting all these people at rush hour? In the middle of the road, in a space left by the crowd on the burning bister pavement, lies a half-naked man. He has been hit by a sand-colored truck. Exhausted and with his face against the road, he is sweating profusely. Fresh blood is trickling from his abdomen. The red of the blood contrasts violently with his anthracite-black skin. He is a fellow of medium build with a rather high forehead and a few scattered hairs on his skull, the probable result of premature baldness. It is just past noon.

FILTHY ASKAR

Filthy Askar (that's his name) died, we are told, on the stretcher of the ambulance that was carrying him to Bourhan Bey hospital.

The crowd disintegrates in silence. Without saying a word, all return to their preoccupations. Only one ragged old woman, more attentive than her cohorts, remembers having seen a billy goat as strong as an ox crushed only yesterday at this same spot.

An insidious, sand-filled wind springs up in this populous neighborhood. You can hear the shabby sheets of aluminum that serve as roofs grate, squeal, twist as they rub together. Some fly off, crash to the ground, barely failing, through I don't know what miracle, to injure numerous, idle passersby. It is a sight too familiar to cause any reaction!

Kids continue to run zigzagging in every direction, between narrow streets more sinuous than streams in the Amazon. The minaret of the white-washed mosque towers over these huts with their motley geometric shapes. Cursed be the Yemeni carpenters who popularized this style! The shacks in question, made of sheet metal, wood, cardboard, and other objects having sojourned in the communal dump—like this automobile chassis repainted with the colors of the shack that it covers—are heaped one on the other and lined up quite clumsily. Between these rows are muddy alleys modestly labeled "streets" (some sport half-erased numbers).

Every morning as the horizon appears, the harmonious and majestic voice of the muezzin rises in a sky still littered with stars. This lyrical voice that invites the faithful to dawn prayers gives the signal to the nocturnal merrymakers to slink off like hyenas to their dens. Tomorrow at sunrise, they will pray in this mosque over the remains of Filthy Askar before burying him in a dark corner of the cemetery.

Of course, the inhabitants of the Samaleh neighborhood are in charge of crying, singing, celebrating this native son before abandoning him in a dark hole of the dusty cemetery. And even my perverse spirit would be unable to summon an undertaker, for the good and simple reason that I know of no such enterprise in this country. Don't look for it, there aren't any!

That old atavistic urge, solidarity, has admirably taken over these tasks for ages.

The common people of the Samaleh neighborhood prepare the funeral ceremonies in a frenzy. The sheikhs take charge of the ablutions; those who were close to Askar attend to wrapping the deceased in his shroud. Everyone recites prayers; for some it is an opportunity to show that they still know their verses. Certainly, the populace celebrates the event in its own way. And for good reason, the most illustrious inhabitants work together: D. B. John, the soul of the neighborhood, has composed a long elegiac poem that begins with these unforgettable words:

> "Askar Harr*
> O Czar! O Star!"

Ardôss, the ingenious dunce, has gotten together a group of young people who volunteer to carry the coffin on their shoulders to the rocky cemetery, and to provide the multitudes with drinking water. The eloquent Joe Joubb, elementary schoolteacher by profession, for whom words are an intimate part of life, was careful to pluck the heartstrings of the populace in the laudatory speech that he justifiably entitled "Askar the Fool, Askar the Sage."

A bit later, Chireh, the bleary-eyed blind patriarch, lips flecked with foam, told of the hectic life of the unruly child who became a quiet—often mute—tramp, and the crowd listened with tears in its eyes. Finally, a young man, whose thick glasses did not fail to attract the attention of the funeral crowd, stood up to announce his plans to write a biography of the late Askar. Several women move heaven and earth to ensure that this sad ceremony is a complete success. Escort our Askar like a prince, they say. All the way to his final resting place. Among these courageous women, there are two in particular: Awo, the poetess-priestess who went all out to sing Askar's praises by compar-

---

Harr means "excrement" in Somali, whence the title of the story, *Filthy Askar.* Incidentally, Askar Harr really existed. He was a tramp.

ing him in turn to King Solomon, to Sayyid Mohamed Abdille Hassan, as well as to St. Francis of Assisi, and Amina, a lively little woman unequaled in her goodness of heart and her quasi-proverbial generosity. Presently, a young athlete responding to the nickname "The Jersey" suggests organizing a soccer match as a finishing touch for the ceremonies. The idea was welcomed with almost universal approval. Except for Ousmane Dheer, a supposedly moral policeman, who seized upon the idea in order to thunder forth—yet again—against the dissolute morals of today's youth, lacking fear of God and Man.

But just who was this Filthy Askar? We know snatches of his story. We know that he was one of the most brilliant students of the Redeeming Fathers of Our Lady of Dikhil. At that time, as was the custom in this milieu, he bore a Christian name: Amédée. We also know that he read so much that he had become intimate with the works of Charles Péguy, St.-John Perse, and Pierre Teilhard de Chardin. With shaven skull, dressed in shabby but clean clothing, he would take his daily stroll in the Dikhil palm grove, always with a book in hand. The urchins already looked with admiring eyes at this young man, different from the others. The puny boy metamorphosed into a robust student, a bit nearsighted, and of pugnacious character. Then, according to a well-informed source, he had taken his leave to be initiated in "Gourpo" (Europe), where it is said that he encountered personalities of every race, of every religion, of every background. Well-fueled rumors hold that he left behind some trace of his passage, implying that he had abandoned an offspring! Years passed. During the struggle for Independence, we heard of him again, because he fought actively for freedom. Many times, he had been thrown into prison. Each time he returned more determined, reinvigorated. He knew that victory was imminent. With some brilliance, he described the luminous tomorrows, with justice and equality for all. Much later, we learned that he had strangely aged and that he had acquired too much deadly fat: Askar was sinking into the labyrinth of oblivion and the murky waters of indifference and sweet insanity. It was probably during this period that people stuck him with the nickname that he dragged like a ball and chain in his descent to hell.

Askar is the double that we hate because we are scared to death of becoming like him. Askar is a strange mirror into which we look from an angle. Now that he is dead, parts of his body will judge him before God. His spinal column will tell how Askar did not lift a finger to bring it some semblance of comfort. One eye will tell how he favored the other; a leg will claim that it often went on strike because he was always limping. For a venial sin, he will cross the Acheron—I know what I'm saying, since I took the same route. That is why I speak in the past, as you may have noticed.

But today, on the occasion of his death, the populace weaves crowns for him, frantically celebrating his ephemeral glory in the patina of his days. The multitude maintains his legend so as to nourish his myth later on. Askar was said to have spoken every language; for some he was above all an engineer, for others a Christ figure . . . In short, his story has only just begun.

A FAINT HOPE

"The man carries a jerrican and an old transistor. He walks in front, climbing the rocky slope with a quick step, heedless of the morning sun that hammers the reddened flanks of the hill. A woman and three children trot along behind, single file, a sack of rice and cloth bundles thrown over their shoulders. Below, at their feet, the bay of Obock scintillates with its white houses, its motionless dhows, and its deserted jetty. The five fugitives do not bother glancing at it . . ."*

The legend of the evil eye exists in all the languages of the world. There they were, their ankles bloody, restless with impatience. The populace had dreamed of taking over the halls of power just as in the past lowly black slaves had risen up in Port-au-Prince, in Haiti.

Time, that great cripple, resumes its indeterminate course. The population is weary and indifferent. No commotion, no clamor. No ululations from the elated good women. A fortress of fear seems to have closed in upon them.

They were dripping with sweat. That is because the incandescence of our noontides is beyond tolerance. Catastrophe had barely been avoided.

Between two pauses, the neighborhood idiot told me, "If troubles persist, we would have to find an amulet to protect us against stray bullets."

I agree with him, try to reassure him. For the thirtieth time, he tells me about what happened yesterday. He tells me how the rank and file stormed the dark velvet padded walls of power, how it almost collapsed, how the crowd had been thirsty for blood . . .

*Le Monde, November 26, 1991. Catherine Simon, a foreign correspondent, covered the civil war in the north of the republic of Djibouti.

He gets excited, agitated, radiant, he rises and gesticulates . . . Who was it who said that condemnation by the people is final? No quarter, everything goes. Everything is carried away . . . He describes the imaginary scene to me: the former leaders thrash about like fish out of water; the agony of whales and the sinuous shudders of eels. Hats, tarbooshes, and fezzes lie on the ground and no one thinks of picking them up . . . He sits down, takes a deep breath, lets his shoulders droop, and for the first time looks at me with placated eyes. Like the rest of the neighborhood, the idiot experiences a moment of fear mingled with a moment of euphoric hope and a moment of absolute anguish.

Time, that eternal cripple, always catches everyone, even crowned heads. Haile Selassie, emperor of Ethiopia, sneaked off in a banal little Volkswagen one September day in 1974.

The idiot told me:

"Stalin's mouthpieces sound off in the hinterland. But who will invent the laxative to heal us of our despair, we who are wedged between barren gravel and incandescent sun? Who will guide us to the ranch of insane hope? Will we ever stop harming each other, stop killing each other? Even before we were born, Cassandras were predicting anarchy, anemia, and the destruction of civil war . . ."

Then, like a lizard that burrows under a stone to flee the burning sand, he disappeared. The circle of seasons has ceased to caress this country of lava flowers. We are relishing this respite.

The idiot told me:

"As for me, I have the taste of rusted metal in my mouth; that's why I assume responsibility for everything I say."

Like the soft, oblong matter that comes out of an anus, he sits down. He is dripping with sweat. He seems to be thirsty.

The idiot told me:

"The populace can stare wide-eyed all it likes, it still won't see any further signs in the course of days to come."

Like a lamb living its last moments in the pool of its ritual blood, he calms down, then weaves a thread of voice that seems like a long sigh.

The idiot told me:

"We had the rhetoric, you felt the shock. There are twenty years of doubt and division between us. You were born with Independence; it made me indolent. Together we await the often trumpeted renaissance . . . (*Deafening silence.*) Democracy is breaking out before our very eyes in certain corners of Africa; will the graft survive? The temptation is too great, to the point that some fools blithely return through the gate of exile and already see themselves replacing the disgraced leader of yesterday. But after such bloodthirsty generals as Idi Amin or Siad Barre, will Africa painfully give birth to the figure of the technocrat, an accountant of frustrations and aspirations? Will the new men in power be better inspired than their predecessors?"

The flaccid specter of uncertainty hovers over the neighborhood. Burning tension reigns over the entire city. The mouthpieces of Stalin sound off in the hinterland, prey to famine. No amnesty on this day. Like a column dropped from the sky, like a vigorous Apollo descended from his belvedere, he stood tall before me.

The idiot told me:

"This country is not a whore."

VORTEX

1. *"Somalia: Hundreds of Refugees Drown.*
Hundreds of Somali refugees are said to have drowned while trying to reach the coast of Yemen after jumping off a boat diverted toward the coasts of that country." (*Ouest-France,* June 24, 1992)

The human condition is at its worst. To express an extreme disgust of distress and to name life where it is found. He is not the first to have taken this route. His savanna-colored eyes, his sooty skin tone: he is a real wild beast from Gehenna, a veritable bird of ill omen: the oracle who predicts the end of Ulysses.

2. *"Somalia: Siad Barre has just renewed the contracts, said to total $600,000, of ten Zimbabwean mercenaries. It will be recalled that in 1988, mercenaries from the former Rhodesia had bombarded northern Somalia."* (*Jeune Afrique Economie,* no. 139, January 1991)

There is a great drought everywhere. A desiccation of the body but also of the mind, one that divides members of the same family. He is separated from his brother, he saw his father and elder sister die. His family carried away by the vortex of destiny. A sign of this: the drought began on the same or almost the same day (I am not about to quibble over a day, you understand) as the great war. The most deadly that has ever been known here below.

3. *"In Somalia especially, but also in Sudan and in Ethiopia, there is no longer a State, no longer an army, no longer any police. In order to get around with a minimum of security, we must hire armed guards,"* said a coordinator of AICF. (*Ouest-France,* June 20–21, 1992)

VORTEX

Even the dogs are quiet. They no longer bark up any trees because they must save their strength. They must walk, walk, all the way to the aid stations. Barking no longer has any meaning. They must walk, walk, walk.

4. Diminuendo.

"Downtown is nothing but a pile of ruins. A pile of rocks crossed by a demarcation line that separates subclans. . . . It is Beirut at the height of the war." A reporter from Radio-France. (*Ouest-France,* ibid.)

He reasons with himself in vain to remain stoic—he is unable to find an acceptable, even bearable, outcome for his life. The solutions that present themselves converged invariably on the same conclusion, the same and only end: his death. The cries of alarm multiply. Yesterday, a black crow predicted a tragic end for him. This afternoon a serpent (a boa constrictor or a python?) spoke to him like a malicious Pythian priestess. He who lives shall see.

5. Continuo.

"They are at the end of their rope. They eat anything. They unearth old piles of garbage. I saw children slip into tanneries to obtain skins. They boil them to make them tender, then they chew them, suck on them. . . ." The same reporter (*Ouest-France,* ibid.)

Did he have a choice? Who had a choice? Even the dogs were silent. Nevertheless, there remain plenty of things for him to see, plenty of books to read, plenty of graves to dig or to watch over, plenty of girls to kiss, plenty of babies to care for. The country has been despoiled, dismembered, desiccated. He is dis-patriated. Nevertheless there remain so many things to do: take care of the babies, help the columns of foreign aid workers distribute food, medicine, set up tents; also to act as an interpreter because he speaks four European languages with ease. Act as an interpreter. As for the rest—the moment of his death, that is—that will have to wait.

6. Piccolo.

"Somalia: a family. The father went insane following a bombardment. From being a victim, he must become an agent of his own evil. In the image of Mogadishu, where everyone ends up by activating evil. In order to survive, one must do evil unto others," reports a photographer. (*L'Evénement du Jeudi*, May 21–27, 1992)

Hell is not in the future, he says to himself, hell is here. Hell is where I live, he continues, before my eyes, in the eyes of my kin, those who died for a thousand unheard of reasons, like those shut away in the edifices of their fears. Like those processing into the foreign aid centers. Hell is an impregnable fortress, an unconquerable virus. It is Gehenna in the tropics where Hades, Satan, and their associates dance. It is Carnival behind the masks of Ogun, Baron Samedi, and the fat Mamawata. After fire comes flood, or rather its opposite, drought:

"No rain this year. Famine settles into the villages where many storehouses are already empty . . . the population compares this famine to the one in 1949 that killed many and prompted many men to leave the country," states a White Father. (*Ouest-France*, June 20–21, 1992)

7. Interlude.

There was
the cry of the tribe facing the mountain
a god cremator of treasures at our doors
and then you in the odor of sacrifice
impossible sister lover
reigning over a closed garden.
—Rabah Belamri, *L'Olivier boit son ombre*

8. Finale.

"In the Horn of Africa, all the great humanitarian organizations are present. Doctors without Borders quickly sounded the alarm regarding Somalia. The AICF has opened eleven feeding stations. Catholic Aid and La Cimade, long present in

VORTEX

Africa, also solicit your generosity." (*Ouest-France,* June 20–21, 1992)

Now he had finished the greatest part of his work. He had taken care of dying babies, he had buried hundreds of victims, he had sung and read as well. He had carefully avoided kissing any girls. He had acted as an interpreter for many an organization. He had done far too much work. It was now up to him to decide what was to follow in the events of his life . . . One sepia-colored morning, under the punctual sun, he took his own life.

NABSI

To a knowledge of rebirth and a promise of tomorrows and tomorrows and an ever beginning of tomorrows.
—Wole Soyinka, "Purgatory," *A Shuttle in the Crypt*

A mercurial night, a country with no family. The wind blows like a dream. Only silence, armor of the weak, remains, when it can be approached. The wind whispers nothing to anyone and dismantles a narrative of anxiety. The feverish eyes of children wander in a house with no family. A narcotic incense, the odor of the master, lingers in the alleyways of misfortune.

A mercurial night gives way to a day the color of dross. The general said, "Piss on it, children!" The general reeks of cuttlebone ink. The general poisons the air. The general's head is crosshatched in three dimensions. Life is a drunken boat in the hands of a macoute general. The general avidly drinks his aloe juice. The future is a rotten, blood-flecked orange in the general's hands. The general eats a puree of testicles (of the dissidents) spiced with hot peppers and petroleum before taking to the bush.

The general's face at the bottom of the ditch. A child-soldier pisses to his heart's content on the general's mug. The general had said, "If I go to hell, we'll all go together." A family with no country spits on the general's mug. A country with no family, a thousand clans in rags, saves its tears for fear of thirst. A toad-man splutters blood on the mug of the general with the sea urchin face. An excrement-encrusted flag, testament to the defunct nation, hangs listlessly. An armed dog vomits his bile, his magazine empty. A cadaver, two cadavers (are they two children or a mother and child?) say hello to the asphalt in a

*The Somali word *nabsi* means "misfortune," "ruin," "death" . . .

suspended sentence. Clack! A vulture takes a picture and sends it to its news agency. There he goes, he is running away!

Here and there the sky shits the blood of a bull, and the sun too. A bald and disinherited moon shivers with hunger and cold. Ogun, the god of war, is contrite and defeated. A seer staggers like a blind man. A stunted tree imitates him. The territory of sorrow trembles all over. Noiselessly, a child scratches the earth in order to swallow one, then two fistfuls of brown sand. Tiny stones grate between the half-dozen teeth that dance in the enclosure of his mouth. He spits something out and then swallows the rest. He coughs, then falls asleep. His weight: an arachnid's touch on the earth. A fleece of shadow. An old man is stretched out beside him. A faded cloth is cajoled by the idle wind. A chiseled face coughs. His hands cover his silvery head lying on his worn sandals. His body is on the blink. A castaway sprung from the night of cruelty collapses and falls asleep. The wanderer is dead. The moon sniffles, weary and alone. A woman tries to rise and then collapses on top of her baby. A man opens his mouth, a tooth the color of pus falls out. He takes it and throws if farther off. A webbed foot tramples a ball of spittle. The flies thumb their noses at the smell. The flies are the smile of nausea.

Biafra-Somalia: *nabsi wa mid:**

Harvest of Hate

. . . .
The hearth is pocked with furnacing of teeth
The air is heavy with rise of incense
For wings womb-moist from the sanctuary of nests
Fall, unfledged to the tribute of fire.

Now we pay forfeit on old abdications
The child dares flames his fathers lit
And in the briefness of too bright flares
Shrivels a heritage of blighted futures
. . . .

—Wole Soyinka, *Idanre and Other Poems*

*Somali for "same misfortune," "same iniquitous destiny."

RETURN

Tribal horror and traces of inhumanity in decrepit landscapes. The sun roasts disjointed shapes. Hillocks afflict the naked savanna: cemeteries that look like termite mounds. Bones, man or bird, decalcify regardless. A young and decomposed woman nibbles on a femur. The bowels of an ass pass from one hand to the other. Knucklebones are crunched with conviction. Without rancor, the heart of the earth wants to smile here, but it is unable to do so. A man passes mechanically in front of the futile boughs that serve as a shelter; he looks at the immobile bodies under the shelter. His gaze catches a ray of sunlight. The boughs utter a barely perceptible litany. But the wind will not say a word to the man. Neither will the wind touch the shelter that spirals inward. Torpor settles over the shelter. Leaves fall and swim in the gravel. Leaves fall. A man also falls. Some children recently grew feathers and no longer fall. That people fall here, isn't it inevitable?

Landscape dilapidated by tribal horror. Traces of inhumanity.

Death froths here and there, reefs of bare bones in the flatness of the plain. There, reefs of bones stiff among the algae of those who foundered in the ocean. The country leafless as far as the eye can see, here and there all the way from Mogadishu the Moor. The city is currently the flower of the liquid ruin of an entire country plunged into darkness. The country has become a Barbary Coast: internecine war is prosperous and highly respected.

A compilation of *technicals* in the arteries of what remains of the capital. The *technicals*—vehicles bristling with automatic weapons, the tanks of the poor—frolic in front so that no one can get through. The "Mad Maxes" are in command of the ruins. A few dollars per man (armed) and per day to protect the *médecins français,* who ensure a meager sustenance. The warlords are proud of them, they operate the *checkpoints.* CARE, Doctors without Borders, AICF, and others maintain the carousel of aid. Save the Children transports children to the *feeding centers.* Villa Somalia—the palace of the Ubuesque dictator—is a mass of shapeless ruins, the last lion having been lapidated by the furious populace. CONCERN relieves CARE, Doctors without Borders backs up AICF. The *gunmen* supply the sorry excuse for a hospital with wounded twenty-four hours a day. Each new day (made by God) falconers bring fresh meat to the doctors.

The frail figures aren't even waiting for Godot any longer, no, they are waiting for the deadly fairy who paces back and forth in front of the clan's enclosure. They wait for the packets of rice sent by French schoolchildren, they wait for the cans of powdered milk, the bottles of oil, some salt, some sugar. At the port, they are apparently even unloading bags of white flour. Someone said that cans of tomato paste are going to arrive soon. The debonair truck drivers condescend to get down from their cabs. They pass out cigarettes from beside their trucks or come to shake hands with the sweating "Mad Maxes."

Has this country signed a pact with Satan? The irony of the situation: people are ripping each other's entrails out in a country where kinship is omnipresent. Irony of language: blood "brothers" who disembowel one another or "brothers" in arms for a fratricidal cause?

A battle of life and death. Death trumpeting from atop a pedestal. Life knocked senseless, rolling on the ground. Life left at death's door. And no one to mourn life as in the old days. Are there no longer any really great men here? In Mogadishu as in Monrovia, as in Khartoum, Luanda, or Djibouti, people search everywhere for the spirit of union. The same credo is uttered everywhere:

My brother before my first cousin
My first cousin before my cousin
My cousin before my ally
My ally before those across from me
Those across from me before my current enemy
My current enemy before my perennial enemy
And everyone, of course, after me.

INTIMATE AND COLOSSAL FRAGMENTS

1. Fragments of a city:

It is night at noon; the days are strung out like beads on a chaplet. The sun completes its great rape: it is all-powerful . . . Life is a halo, then a shade. Grandmother said that God had ordered the sea never to cross its boundary so as not to trouble men. Since then, the inclemency of days grows with each stitch of night just like this continuously unraveling social fabric. Grandmother said that gone was the time when one scratched one's head outside the boutiques selling great bags of wood charcoal and small bags of frozen water. Here at home vigorous soldiers from a far-off Occident strut before their square receivers. Grandmother would have quoted this line from Léon Bloy—if she hadn't died the summer before the arrival of the boys from the Dakotas: "We would be able to lick each other and lick our lips to our content, titivate our suckers and caress our proboscises and congratulate our appendixes in the corners of sacristies colonized by cockroaches." And she would have been right. Here at home, in front of the red-faced men from Montana, Bush came to sip a Coke while stroking his chin. The local caudates only had one thing to say: "Thank you! Thank you!" The flock of journalists had smiles on their faces. Grandmother was no longer there. How to render this hope postponed indefinitely?

2. Fragments of a letter (translated from Somali):

"We celebrated the feast of Mawled. We slaughtered some sheep. The schoolchildren came to share the food with us. Everyone in the village was happy and the mothers laughed a lot in the school kitchen. The men arrived accompanied by the sheikhs and the sheikhs recited some hadiths. We sang the name of the prophet Muhammad. Next we sowed a lot of seeds and the garden is full of green vegetables, bananas, and millet.

INTIMATE AND COLOSSAL FRAGMENTS

Thank you very much, my sponsors, and the association 'Enfance et partage.'
Your adoptive son,
Cabdi."

3. Fragment of a newspaper article:
"And yet, two years ago, almost to the day, January 11, 1991, Halima, the eldest, age forty-eight, who always covers her head with the shaash, the red or black turban that married women must wear all their lives, saw her spouse, a manufacturer, abducted from their residence. It was the eve of the fall of the dictator Siad Barre. The next day, Halima roamed the city looking for her husband. Finally, an imam told her where the body was located, because Siad Barre's men had assassinated him. . . . Since the beginning of the civil war two years ago, Leila knows only misfortune and sorrow. Her husband is a refugee in a camp in Kenya. He did not abandon her. Neither of them wanted to abandon their clan, preferring it to the family, while waiting for 'better days' perhaps." (Julia Ficatier, *La Croix,* December 1993)

4. Fragment of a phrased discourse:
"What is unreal today is real tomorrow."—John Coltrane
It is night at noon. The noctules fly away toward a deserted sky, streaked but cloudless. A sky becoming to the landscape here below. What is there to understand anyway when even Grandmother admits that everything is beyond her understanding? Night invades day and takes on diurnal traits. Strange bonds are woven before our eyes. A rock devours a rock, men have been left to live in apnea on dry land—only the serenely insane feel secure there. The unreality of the insane is the certainty of tomorrow. We must confront the immensely cemented sky: a sky that no longer carts clouds. A sky with sanious spots under which we must learn the craft of being men. We will begin by making ours the art of the fragment because life is too complex to be seized in its entirety. By parasitizing, cannibalizing official discourses, be they by experts or from the media, by

dispensing them *in naturabilus.* By reducing them to percussive echoes in this world where indignation is calculated according to suffering. One does not look a gift horse in the mouth: is that really the moral of the American intervention in this country where the loss of love between Somali clans rages? Those responsible are just the very ones—local warlords but also the Organization of African Unity, the regional powers and their immediate interests, etc.—who would like to hide behind the fig leaf of their ignorance.

5. Fragment of a desert fragment:
The nomad knows and admires for its endurance that little sand-colored animal, the fox. The fox—or fennec—so thin, more famished than a flea on a bald man's head, demands respect. The oryx seeks him out but fears him, man strokes him with his gaze but is jealous of him. Thick plants aid his passage and the stars accompany him when night falls. His silence is a discourse, his gaze at once sharp and panoramic. The fox in the desert is the untiring man who wears down the horizon. What can man do against this indomitable other? Will he not encounter this double in his final dwelling place? The fox is the man who flees death, but that cannot be since "every man will taste death." (*Qur'an,* 2:185)

6. Fragment of a monologue or agony:
Anâ Ahya? Am I alive? *Wal layali?* And the nights? Does the sky exist? Zero—*as sifr*—does it mean anything? And the inclemency of nights and days? Why am I living here permanently? So just where is the suicide room? Isn't it true that the dead are oriented toward the *quibla,* Mecca? One whispers the *shahada,* doesn't one? But where are those who are supposed to watch over my death? *Naf eey!*
A long silence unfurls con-ti-nu-ous-ly.

GLOSSARY

Abdelkadir Jilani: a Somali saint

ACCT: Agence de Coopération Culturelle et Technique (Cultural and Technical Cooperation Agency)

AICF: Action Internationale contre la Faim (International Action against Hunger)

Aïd: the feast that follows the fast of Ramadan

Edicef: Editions Classiques d'Expression Française (Classic Editions of French Expression)

Lesseps, Ferdinand de (1805-94): French engineer and designer of the Suez and Panama canals

La Cimade: Association Oecuménique d'Entraide (Ecumenical Mutual Aid Association)

Mawled: celebration of the birth of the Prophet Muhammad

Naf eey: cry of agony

Orgabo: Ethiopian tribe living in the Awash valley

Sallawaad: "Heaven forbid"

shahada: Muslim profession of faith

Soub'han'Allah: "By Allah the Perfect"

CARAF Books

Caribbean and African Literature
Translated from French